Informal Learning Basics

Saul Carliner

ASTD
PRESS

Alexandria, Virginia

ASTD Press is an internationally renowned source of insightful and practical information on workplace learning and performance topics, including training basics, evaluation and return on investment, instructional systems development, e-learning, leadership, and career development. Visit us at www.astd.org/astdpress.

Ordering information: Books published by ASTD Press can be purchased by visiting ASTD's website at store.astd.org or by calling 800.628.2783 or 703.683.8100.

Library of Congress Control Number: 2010938802

ISBN-10: 1-56286-785-7
ISBN-13: 978-1-56286-785-0

ASTD Press Editorial Staff:
Director: Anthony Allen
Manager, ASTD Press: Glenn Saltzman
Community Manager, Learning and Development: Juana Llorens
Associate Editor: Ashley McDonald
Associate Editor: Stephanie Castellano
Copyediting, Interior Design, and Production: Abella Publishing Services, LLC
Cover Design: Ana Foreman

Printed by Versa Press, Inc., East Peoria, IL, www.versapress.com

Contents

iii

About the *Training Basics* Series

ASTD's *Training Basics* series recognizes and, in many ways, celebrates the fast-paced, ever-changing reality of organizations today. Jobs, roles, and expectations change quickly. One day you might be a network administrator or a process line manager, and the next day you might be asked to train 50 employees in basic computer skills or to instruct line workers in quality processes.

Where do you turn for help? The ASTD *Training Basics* series is designed to be your one-stop solution. The series takes a minimalist approach to your learning curve dilemma and presents only the information you need to be successful. Each book in the series guides you through key aspects of training: giving presentations, making the transition to the role of trainer, designing and delivering training, and evaluating training. The books in the series also include some advanced skills such as performance and basic business proficiencies.

The ASTD *Training Basics* series is the perfect tool for training and performance professionals looking for easy-to-understand materials that will prepare non-trainers to take on a training role. In addition, this series is the perfect reference tool for any trainer's bookshelf and a quick way to hone your existing skills.

Preface

Purpose

This book discusses informal learning as it applies to training and development professionals who would like to leverage it to help workers perform their jobs.

The definition of informal learning as proposed by this book is a pragmatic one, referring to informal learning as situations in which some combination of the process, location, purpose, and content of instruction are determined by the worker, who may or may not be conscious that an instructional event occurred. This view of informal learning encompasses a range of activities, from highly structured on-the-job training to the often unplanned or impromptu steps that some workers take to further their careers.

The discussion that follows takes a similarly pragmatic approach, presenting the benefits and drawbacks of informal learning processes and a framework for integrating informal learning into a complete training and development program throughout the life span of a job.

To help readers apply this framework, this book then explores issues involved in promoting informal learning in the workplace, including gaining support for learning, opportunities for informal learning that are already present in the workplace, technologies that support informal learning, and means of evaluating informal learning.

Who Should Read This Book

The primary readers of this book are training and development professionals in all roles—instructors, instructional designers, administrators, managers, and executives—who have experience with formal learning programs and have been asked to explore or implement informal learning in their organizations.

Secondary readers are managers and professionals in other disciplines who are concerned about ways to prepare workers for their jobs and careers outside formal training programs.

Look for These Icons

What's Inside This Chapter

Each chapter of this book begins with a preview of the topics to be discussed in the chapter. Use this information to help you determine which parts of the chapter are most valuable to you.

Think About This

These notes will expand on or reinforce important concepts in each chapter. They may contain actionable advice or simply recall valuable information from previous chapters.

Basic Rule

These rules summarize powerful concepts and knowledge brought forth by the book. They'll help you skim a chapter to glean the information most important to you.

Noted

These sections include important additional information that slightly digresses from the regular text.

Getting It Done

This is the final section of each chapter. It contains worksheets and exercises that will reinforce what you learned in the chapter and help you apply that knowledge to your own workplace.

Acknowledgments

■ ■

Like any book, this one represents a collaboration among many people. It started with two accidents. The first occurred in May 2010, when the Canadian Society for Training and Development needed a last-minute replacement for the speaker on informal learning at its spring symposium. A family emergency prevented Christine Wihak from presenting. Because I had reviewed the report on her research on informal learning for the Work and Learning Knowledge Centre of the former Canadian Council on Learning, CSTD program planner Danielle Lamothe thought of me. Christine generously shared her prepared presentation with me, but partly because I felt guilty presenting someone else's presentation and partly because I hold much passion for the subject, I developed my own materials. So thanks to Danielle and Christine.

The second accident occurred a few months later. Cat Russo of Russo Rights suggested that I contact Justin Brusino at ASTD Press about a matter related to a previously published book. Like much informal learning, our conversation took many unexpected turns—ultimately landing at a request to submit a proposal for this book. So thanks to Cat.

Thanks, too, to Justin for his patience in waiting for the manuscript of this book (which, like most informal learning, was delivered on its own schedule) and to Mark Morrow, who provided insightful editorial comments on the first draft.

Several others also provided purposeful input. Tim Walker and Colleen Bernard—PhD students at Concordia University—scanned the literature for me and provided early reviews of the book. Margaret Driscoll, a collaborator on a previous book, provided a sanity check for me.

Thanks to the various locations of Panera and Starbucks, as well as the food courts of *Carrefour Laval, Centre Eaton, Centre Rockland, Complexe Les Ailes, Place Vertu, Mall Champlain,* and *Promenades de la Catedrale* in Montreal for providing work tables, electrical outlets, and free WiFi so that I had friendly, quiet retreats where I could research and write this book.

Special thanks go to Stephanie Castellano for her collaboration on the final drafts of the book. She not only tightened up the entire book, she brought me perspective on the content at a time when I had lost it.

Last, thanks to my partner Marco Manrique for saint-like patience while I spent evenings, nights, weekends, and holidays researching and writing this book.

Introduction

■ ■

Great things happen when young people discover their life calling while exploring their passions. Consider how a visit to a museum affected Diane Ackerman, author of *A Natural History of the Senses*:

> I was 17 years old the first time I entered the American Museum of Natural History in New York. I knew nothing about its layout or holdings at the time, so it was pure serendipity that led me to one of the lower levels on Central Park West. There I drifted into a small, quiet gallery and stood in front of a display of microscopic invertebrates, the creatures that inhabit the minute wetlands of our lives. . . . I felt so startled by joy that my eyes teared. It was a spiritual experience of power and clarity; limning the wonder and sacredness of life, life at any level, even the most remote. . . . I was. . . .feeling saturated by wonder. Only praise leapt to mind, praise that knows no half-truths and pardons all. I felt what Walt Whitman may have felt when he wrote of the starry night, "The bright suns I see and the dark suns I cannot see are in their place." His intuition bespeaks the cryptic faith in the unknown and the extrapolation of belief that organized religions require. The part stands for the whole, as it does in natural history museums that say, in effect, "Here is one wildebeest on the savanna, but there are many more of them, it's part of a species. Trust in it." (Ackerman, 1993, pp. 102–103).

Great things can also happen when motivated professionals, working on their own, learn from one another to solve important problems. Consider how partners work together to place the homeless in housing:

The other linchpin of the campaign is encouraging city partners—who participate in weekly webinars and monthly innovation sessions—to teach one another how to get around bottlenecks in government systems. "There's a half dozen things that each community struggles with that somebody has already figured out," explains Kanis. "When you go to your housing authority with an idea they think is crazy, it helps if you can say, 'We're just trying to do what Baltimore did. . . .' It takes away the excuses people have for saying something will never work." (Bornstein, 2010)

Great things also happen, too, when training and development professionals empower workers to succeed on their own, providing them with the learning and support that those learners need at the time they need it. Consider e-learning manager Ryan Tracey's blog post "My Award-Winning IQ."

My driver for creating this [intranet-based] portal was the realisation that, in a big corporation like the one I work for, knowledge is distributed everywhere—on random intranet pages, in obscure folders, in people's heads—which makes it really hard to find.

As an L&D professional, my concern was: If someone wants to learn something, where do they start? (Tracey, 2010)

Each of these examples exhibits an unbridled enthusiasm for learning, and notice that in not one of them did the participants need a classroom or an instructor. In the field of education, we generally call this type of learning *informal* learning. For those of us who have experienced it (and most of us have), this type of learning feels especially powerful because we initiated it, and we feel a special sense of ownership of the results.

Like Diane Ackerman, I was introduced to informal learning through museums. But unlike Ackerman, facilitating that type of learning became my life's passion, and I eventually chose to conduct my dissertation research on learning in museums. I specifically explored how exhibit designers designed learning into their exhibits, and the study resulted in a grounded model of instructional design for informal learning (Carliner, 1998). I called this project my "hobby dissertation" because I felt that, although the study would fulfill the academic requirements for my degree and nourish my passion, it would have little impact on my professional work.

I couldn't have been more wrong.

What I learned from the museum professionals who informed this study provided both a fundamental understanding of informal learning and, in the process, transformed my understanding of instructional design. Through this book, I hope to share my passion for informal learning with you.

I also hope to share the informal learning principles that the museum exhibit designers who participated in my study taught me, such as ways of generating interest in topics, providing learners with several pathways into—and through—the material, and developing a comfort with learners taking their own lessons away from the experience—ones that differ from the lessons that were intended.

But as I have learned when I focused my later research on the workplace, the nature of informal learning in museums—on which jobs and reputations rarely hang in the balance, and that knows no other schedule than the one imposed by the opening and closing times of the museum—substantially differs from the nature of informal learning in the workplace, where people need to learn content so they can effectively perform their jobs, where learning must often happen on a schedule determined by the employer, and where consequences exist for failing to learn.

So, in addition to building your passion for the subject, I hope to channel it into practical, realistic efforts to engage your organization in informal learning. In this book, I take the position that informal learning complements formal learning, and I explain why informal learning cannot always replace formal instruction.

I also try to build realistic expectations of informal learning for developing work-related knowledge and skills, suggest a framework for integrating informal learning into the development of workers at various phases in their jobs, and explain how to develop an infrastructure of support for informal learning that builds on efforts and initiatives already occurring in your organization. In addition, I describe a variety of group and individual activities that promote informal learning—many of which uncover the learning that takes place during ordinary work activities—and identify technologies that support informal learning. In the last chapter, I discuss means of evaluating informal learning.

In other words, while keeping its "head" in the clouds of passion for informal learning, this book tries to keep its "feet" on the ground, with realistic, practical approaches that most training and development professionals can apply in their own work environments.

What Is Informal Learning?

What's Inside This Chapter

In this chapter, you'll learn

- ▶ what informal learning is
- ▶ how informal learning, nonformal learning, incidental learning, and self-directed learning differ from one another
- ▶ why employers have shown increasing interest in informal learning in the past several years.

Informal Learning in the Workplace

Although the concept of informal learning generates much excitement among training and development professionals, conversations with several of them suggest that what's "informal" to some is not considered informal by others. So before any meaningful discussion of the basics of informal learning can occur, we first need to determine what is and what isn't considered informal learning. This chapter explores this crucial issue in detail, places the current interest in informal learning within a longer history of interest in alternatives to classroom learning, and explains how conditions outside of training are igniting current interest in informal learning.

To start this discussion, consider the following stories of informal learning in different workplaces.

1. Casey—New Assistant Store Manager: To introduce Casey to her new job responsibilities as assistant manager at a clothing store in the shopping mall, the store manager gives Casey a tour of the store, the stockroom in back, and the management office. Then the manager shows her a few popular items in the store, describes how the sales process works, explains policies regarding the fitting room, and shows Casey how to use the cash register. After the tour, the manager sets up Casey on the company intranet and leaves her for a few hours to explore other store policies and procedures. Later in the day, the manager observes Casey as she interacts with customers and completes her first sale.

2. Ricardo—Customer Service Agent: Ricardo has six years' experience as a customer service agent for a major insurance company. Although he is well-versed in the policies and procedures—and laws—governing his job, he has also learned a few tricks that help in particular situations. For example, although the company maintains a list of authorized repair shops that can estimate and complete work on damaged autos, he has heard from customers that some of those repair shops are more reliable than others. So when customers ask him where they can go, he only mentions the names of the shops that have served customers well and avoids telling customers about shops that have high levels of complaints.

3. Curtis—Construction Firm Supervisor: Curtis is a site supervisor for a construction firm. In his management training, the company emphasized the importance of safety and said that managers could fire workers who repeatedly violated safety rules. But when Curtis fires a roofer whose injuries resulted from failing to follow safety rules, he learns from Human Resources (HR) that he should have followed a specific process to fire an employee, and because he did not do so, the company must now fire Curtis for failing to follow their policies.

4. Marley—Ad Agency Executive: Marley is a junior account executive with an advertising agency who takes an unfocused approach to her work, sometimes selling consumer advertising and sometimes selling business-to-business advertising. Another experienced account executive mentors Marley on how to better focus her energies and natural talents toward a single goal—business-to-business sales. Within a year, Marley becomes the account executive with the second highest level of sales in business-to-business advertising.

5. Karin—Software Engineer: Karin is a systems engineer for a software company. She regularly uses the company's sophisticated knowledge base to troubleshoot tough problems and tailor the system to meet the unique needs of her clients. Through trial and error, she has learned which keywords to use with searches so that they provide the most useful results. When she can't find an answer in the knowledge base, Karin sends out a message to other systems engineers through the company's internal social media system. Usually, someone quickly provides an answer and she can solve problems for customers in a timely way.

All of these examples represent informal learning under one definition or another. The first case—Casey—is an example of on-the-job training and provides a structured approach to learning. The second case—Ricardo—is an example of job-related knowledge acquired over time and shared in the context of the job. The third case—Curtis—is an example of learning through trial and error; only by failing did the employee learn the importance of learning company policies before acting. The fourth case—Marley—is an example of learning through mentoring. The last case—Karin—is an example of using online resources, social media, and networks to solve problems.

According to a 2009 Conference Board of Canada study (Bloom, 2009), 56 percent of work-related learning occurs in informal contexts. Other authors, such as Jay Cross (2007), suggest that this percentage is closer to 70 percent. Given these findings, it's no surprise that learning professionals are keenly interested in trying to understand informal learning so they can harness its power in their organizations.

A Definition of Informal Learning

Some definitions of informal learning focus on its learner-controlled nature. For example, my own early definition of informal learning identified it as a process in which learners set their own learning objectives and determined what successful completion would look like. Such a definition is only partially supported by the real world, because some of the learning that we label as "informal" occurs accidentally, as demonstrated by the experience of Curtis the construction manager, or as the result of repeated experiences on the job, such as how Ricardo learned which auto repair shops to recommend.

Other learning that we label as "informal" occurs as the result of purposeful activity—like the example of Casey's on-the-job orientation—or builds on formally acquired knowledge, such as in the example of Karin and her creative solution to software troubleshooting, which was built on her already strong knowledge about the systems she supports. And some informal learning happens through relationships, such as the efforts of Marley and her mentor to focus her efforts toward a single goal.

In other words, formal and informal learning are not necessarily distinct from one another. Victoria Marsick, one of the leading researchers on informal learning, and her colleagues note the interplay of formal and informal learning and point out that "informal and formal learning interact in important ways" (2009).

In fact, some of the strongest definitions of informal learning acknowledge that some aspects of it are formal. Some researchers have likened informal learning to a control panel with "levers," each of which suggests a different type of control over the learning process (Colley, Hodkinson, and Malcolm, 2003; Wihak, et al., 2008). These are the informal learning "levers":

- ▶ **Process:** who controls and assesses learning. In the most formal situations, learning is controlled and defined by the instructor, who establishes objectives and, through assessments, determines whether learners have achieved the objectives. In the least formal situations, learners establish their own objectives and criteria and determine when the learning is complete.
- ▶ **Location:** where the learning occurs. In the most formal situations, learning occurs in a place intended for learning, such as a traditional or virtual classroom. In the least formal situations, learning occurs organically in the context of everyday life.
- ▶ **Purpose:** whether learning is a primary or secondary goal of the learning activity. In the most formal situations, learning is the primary goal. In the least formal situations, learning is an accidental by-product.
- ▶ **Content:** whether the topic of study is for immediate or long-term use. Acquisition of a body of content—such as the concepts underlying an

occupation—tends to have long-term use and is considered more formal, while content about processes and procedures in a particular context has more immediate impact on the job—and in job performance—and is considered more informal.

▶ **Consciousness:** the extent to which learners are aware that learning has occurred. In the most formal situations, learners have a high level of awareness that learning has occurred (or that it should have occurred). In the least formal situations, learners may not even realize that they learned something until long after the experience.

Informal learning, as defined by this book, is based on these levers. See Figure 1–1 for a more graphic representation of the interrelation of these control panel levers.

Figure 1–1. Visual Representation of the Definition of Informal Learning

How Formal Is the Learning?

Process	Location	Purpose	Content	Consciousness
Who controls and assesses the learning process?	Is the place where learning occurred intended for learning?	Is learning a primary or secondary goal of the activity?	Is the content abstract, such as concepts; or practical, related to an everyday skill?	When it happens, are people aware that learning has occurred?

Basic Rule

When this book uses the term *informal learning*, it refers to situations in which some combination of the process, location, purpose, and content of instruction are determined by the worker, who may or may not be conscious that an instructional event has occurred.

Definitions of Other Terms Used for Informal Learning

Although this book has a particular definition for informal learning, as noted earlier, the term is defined in many different ways by training and development profession-als—and many use other terms interchangeably or in conjunction with informal learning, including *nonformal learning, incidental learning, self-directed learning, transfer of training,* and the relatively new *ubiquitous learning.* This confusing termi-nology creates a barrier to meaningful discussions of informal learning because people might use the same terms, but actually mean different things. The following section clears up the confusion by defining these terms and contrasting them with the definition of informal learning.

- ▶ **Formal Learning:** Instruction in which the instructor or some similar "expert" sets the objectives and determines the requirements for successful completion. Examples include classroom instruction, diploma and degree programs, and certificate programs.

- ▶ **Nonformal Learning:** Programs that have learning as one of many primary outcomes or as a secondary outcome. Usually, nonformal learning programs are events, such as lectures, exercise classes, and demonstrations, whose goals are as much social and physical as they are intellectual. They can be offered by community, cultural, educational, religious, and sporting organizations, as well as by employers.

- ▶ **Incidental Learning:** Knowledge and skills acquired unintentionally in situations not formally intended to provide instruction. It is accidental learning in a nonlearning context.

- ▶ **Self-Directed Learning:** Programs of study that workers undertake on their own with the intention of achieving a particular goal. Although workers might initiate, plan, and complete the program on their own, many work with an instructor or similar guide who oversees these activities and prepares a learning contract, which structures the learning and acknowledges successful completion of the program. Examples include on-the-job training, such as the orientation that Casey received on her first day on the job as assistant manager.

- ▶ **Transfer of Training:** Involves a combination of formal and informal activities; formal activities include the availability of follow-up training and access to information and resources, and informal activities include opportunities to perform the skills in a real-world setting, receive feedback on this performance, and reflect privately and with others about what was learned. Although the transfer activities are considered informal, they are associated with a formal training program.

▶ **Ubiquitous Learning:** Situations in which instructional materials are always available and students use the materials as the need arises. Karin's use of the knowledge base is an example of ubiquitous learning. She has access to this knowledge base at all times and uses it for purposes other than strictly learning.

How Has the Concept of Informal Learning Developed Over Time?

Although the contemporary interest in informal learning seems recent to many training and development professionals, specialists in adult and workplace learning have had an interest in the ways that people learn outside of formal settings for decades. Admittedly, the focus and terminology have changed over time. Figure 1–2 shows the evolution in thinking about informal learning, primarily in recent times.

Figure 1–2. The Evolution of Informal Learning

De facto and formal apprentice-ships "School of life"	Self-directed learning	Adult learning theory, human performance technology, computer-based training, and informal (later "free-choice") learning in museums	Electronic performance support systems and *edutainment* (integration of education with entertainment to make learning fun)	Knowledge management (recording and effectively sharing the intellectual property within organizations) and e-learning	Informal learning
Before formal schooling	**1960s and 1970s**	**1970s and 1980s**	**Early 1990s**	**Late 1990s**	**Late 2000s**

New Interest in Informal Learning

Educators and other learning professionals have long been interested in informal learning and, with time, have grown increasingly comfortable using informal learning to meet specific learning demands.

But developments outside the field of training and development, including the changing nature of work, changing views on human resources, and the pervasiveness of technology, are driving the current interest in informal learning. This section presents six trends underlying this interest.

Think About This

The current interest in informal learning results from a confluence of trends, including the rise of technologies like social media, increasingly dynamic work assignments and changing concepts of talent development, and a growing frustration with traditional classroom training.

Trend 1: A Growing Awareness of the Extent of Informally Acquired Knowledge

One of the insights resulting from the research of the past several decades is the recognition of the extent to which workers gain and apply informally acquired knowledge and the role it plays in developing work skills. David Livingstone (2010) and his colleagues at the University of Toronto, who have been tracking informal learning at work for several decades, have consistently found that more than 90 percent of adults participate in some informal learning activities in a given year. Adults do so not only for paid work, but also for volunteer work, housework, and their personal interests.

Some researchers have tried to estimate the amount of work-related learning that happens informally. As noted at the beginning of this chapter, the Conference Board of Canada (Bloom, 2009) reports that 56 percent of work-related learning occurs outside of formal contexts, and other sources peg that number at 70 or even 80 percent. Victoria Marsick (2009) notes, however, that because much of that learning is unconscious, definitively identifying the extent of informal learning on the job raises significant challenges. Instead, in-depth studies provide insights into which types of skills workers learn informally and how they learn them.

Trend 2: Rise of Technologies That Can Support Informal Learning

PCs and networking made on-demand learning and access to information feasible, and the generation of computing that followed further expanded access to online learning materials and information. This next generation of computing also featured simplified designs, so people who do not work as training and development specialists can easily prepare their own instructional and informative materials. Devices like laptop computers, tablets, and smartphones (such as the iPhone) have web access and also provide learners with access to instructional and informative materials wherever their devices can find a signal (or anywhere, if the materials are stored directly on their devices).

Several newer software applications have simplified the task of publishing materials. Blogs let individuals easily publish articles on the Internet. Wikis let groups collaborate on a single document. Microblogging sites (for example, Twitter) and other social networking venues (for example, LinkedIn and Facebook) link people with common interests and allow them to publish and share instructional and informative materials. Microblogging and social networking also provide opportunities for people to discuss these materials and related issues, thus furthering their learning.

Specialized software for learning also helps workers publish their own instructional and informative materials. Learning content management systems can provide templates (similar to fill-in-the-blank forms) that guide subject matter experts (SMEs) through the process of providing material on a given subject so that it contains all of the information that workers need.

Receiving less notice is the significant growth in the power of the Internet and the amount of storage available on most of the devices on it, which allows systems to provide more material and in an increasing variety of ways. Increased availability of storage has resulted not only in a switch to new materials being published online rather than in print (or in addition to print), but also in the digitization of materials published in the past, so that learners have access to entire libraries of information online. At first, most online material was only available in text format. By the 1990s, text expanded to include photos and illustrations. By the late 2000s, text, photos, and illustrations expanded to include audio recordings, videos, and live voice. As a result, even television broadcasters are distributing their programs on the Internet.

Note that with the exception of the live virtual classroom, all of this technology promotes learner-initiated and learner-controlled activities.

Trend 3: Increasingly Dynamic, Knowledge-Based Work Assignments

In addition to promoting learning online, making vast quantities of materials available, and linking users, computerization has also affected the nature of work. Because computers provide decision makers with information more quickly, and with a pinpoint focus not otherwise feasible, they have helped organizations develop sophisticated business strategies that let them better target their activities and respond more quickly to external events. This, in turn, has resulted in a greater flexibility of work assignments (Jacobs and Park, 2009).

This increased flexibility takes many forms. One is more flexible work teams that bring together people with the expertise needed on a particular project and then disband when workers have completed the project. Another is shorter product development cycles. Projects that once took one to five years now take three months to one year. Along with this flexibility comes the expectation that workers become productive more quickly on projects, because organizations have less time to devote to training workers.

The need to develop knowledge and skills as fast as possible poses a couple of practical challenges. In some instances, the training programs that could develop this knowledge and skill are not scheduled when workers need them. In other instances, the knowledge and skills needed are so specialized that, even if a class could be scheduled, few people would have the expertise to design and develop the program. This ushers in the need for informal learning programs.

Trend 4: Changing Concepts of Talent Development

As a by-product of this changing nature of work, organizations have changed their strategies for recruiting and retaining workers, an endeavor known as *talent development*. In the past, employers hired workers with the intention of employing them for the long term. Workers were rewarded for their loyalty with raises, promotions, and job transfers. To support this process, employers provided extensive developmental opportunities to their workers, including training, job rotations, and career planning in an effort to help workers contribute to the organization in the long term.

In the early 1990s, significant changes occurred to this widely understood, though unwritten, "contract" with workers. As business globalized, competition increased, and work became increasingly project focused and short term, organizations sought increasing levels of flexibility in meeting these factors. Rather than hiring a worker for life and promoting based on *seniority* (the number of years a worker has been employed by an organization), the *new employment contract*, as some called it, involved organizations hiring workers for their skills and retaining and promoting them based on the need for their skills by the organization, also called the *protean career*. Some advocates of this approach (such as Peter Cappelli, 2008) even advise organizations to focus most of their formal training efforts on the top performers to be retained. Organizations should only provide the rest of their workers with essential training needed to complete the job.

The practical implication of this development is that many organizations have shifted hiring strategies from a focus on full-time workers to a focus on hiring temporary ones. Partly because of business demand and partly because of tax codes in many countries, these temporary workers are expected to have all of the skills needed for their assignments. Many employers have cut back or eliminated formal training in occupational classes where the majority of workers are temporary, or in those occupations not deemed critical to the organization.

As a result, workers are left to develop and maintain their skills on their own—and pay for it out of their own pockets. Surveys show that independent workers in even fast-changing fields are relying on informal learning to build their skills (Lalonde, 2010). To verify whether workers actually have these skills, both workers and employers increasingly turn to external certification programs (Carter, 2005; Werquin, 2007), as certification programs are intended not only to demonstrate familiarity with a body of knowledge, but more significantly, competence in a certain occupation. Recognizing that people can only develop so much work-related competence in the classroom, many certification programs include a *residency requirement*, that is, a requirement to have completed a designated number of years working in the field, before candidates can apply for certification.

Trend 5: Frustration With Formal Learning

One of the primary drivers of interest in informal learning is a frustration with the dominant alternative, formal learning.

One source of frustration with formal learning is the quality of classroom courses. Some studies have shown that the content of training courses fails to meet the needs of the organization sponsoring them or the learners taking them. Many formal courses rely on instructor-delivered lectures (as noted in every ASTD *State of the Industry Report*), which are assumed to be unsatisfactory learning experiences.

Scheduling is another common frustration with formal instruction. Because the students and instructor must participate at the same time, and organizations only hold classes when a certain minimum number of people enroll, courses might not be available when learners need the content.

Even when scheduling works, classes usually involve many ancillary costs, yet another frustration with formal learning. One such cost is travel, because training classes are often held off site, sometimes requiring extensive travel. Another is salary for the work time spent in training (and travel to training). Workers often receive salary for training time, although they are not performing immediately "productive" work. The live virtual classroom, in which instructor-led sessions occur online using online meeting software like Webex and Connect, addresses some concerns about travel costs. But employers and instructors alike wonder whether learners are really paying attention to these online classes.

Trend 6: Long-Term Shifts in Spending on Training

ASTD's annual *State of the Industry* reports have found that the total percentage of instructor-led training between 2003 and 2009 remained nearly unchanged, at approximately 70 percent of all training, although the percentage offered through live virtual classrooms increased from approximately 2 to 6 percent.

However, research also shows that overall use of formal learning is declining. For example, an analysis of spending on workplace learning in the United States between 1986 and 2008 showed that, after adjusting for inflation, employer spending on training has essentially remained flat over the entire period and declined since the dot-com bubble burst in 2000 (Carliner and Bakir, 2010). When factoring in growth of the workforce, spending per worker actually fell more than 30 percent. The need for learning did not decline with the spending; one possible explanation for the decline is that workers are learning informally.

In addition, as noted in the last section, workers are assuming responsibility for their skill and career development, and surveys of their behavior suggest that these workers prefer to do it through informal learning.

Furthermore, the frustration with classroom training is leading some training and development professionals to experiment with different approaches to workplace learning and performance. Many of these prototype projects are structured partially or fully around informal learning.

Most significantly, even the staunchest advocates of classroom training agree that without efforts outside the classroom—that is, informal learning—the training has a low likelihood of transferring to the job. This is the underlying focus of strengthening training transfer efforts. As the evidence for that point of view mounts, the importance of informal learning becomes increasingly difficult to overlook.

How Does This Book Assist You in Providing and Promoting Informal Learning in Your Organization?

Exploring ways to weave formal and informal learning together to support skill and professional development in the workplace is the goal of this book. When discussing informal learning, I focus on practical approaches that either have demonstrated success in the workplace or have a high likelihood of doing so.

The next two chapters provide descriptions of how informal learning can be integrated into the workplace. Chapter 2 briefly summarizes key principles of informal learning that should guide any consideration of its use in the workplace. It describes not only the potential and benefits, but also some of the pitfalls of informal learning that research has identified. Chapter 3 suggests a framework for integrating both formal and informal learning at each phase or *touchpoint* in the life span of a worker's tenure in a job. In doing so, the chapter suggests that informal learning already exists in most workplaces; but most organizations do not use it as effectively as they could.

The rest of the chapters of this book explain how to make the most effective use of informal learning. Because informal learning already exists in the workplace, these chapters approach it from the perspective of how to leverage informal learning opportunities that already exist and expand their use, rather than launching a new program. Each of the chapters describes a different type of "tool" used in supporting informal learning. Chapter 4 explains how to promote and support informal learning at the individual and organizational levels before, during, and after learning experiences. Chapter 5 inventories informal learning experiences that involve two or more people. Chapter 6 inventories individual learning experiences. Chapter 7 explores how to use technology to provide and support informal learning. Chapter 8 describes the challenges in evaluating informal learning, and then suggests a model and some practical techniques you can use to assess both the extent and the effectiveness of informal learning in your organization.

These discussions assume that you are an experienced training and development professional who either has executive or management responsibility, serves as a performance consultant or curriculum planner, or is a veteran of designing or teaching several training and development programs. If you do not have experience as a training and development professional, you might consider reading these ASTD Press books: *Adult Learning Basics* to become familiar with the principles of adult learning as they relate to workplace learning, *Telling Ain't Training* to become familiar with the role of training in developing and validating skills and knowledge, and *Training Design Basics* to familiarize yourself with the process of designing and developing training programs.

Getting It Done

Before training and development professionals can effectively provide and promote informal learning for others, they need an awareness of their own interests in, and preferences for, informal learning. This activity is intended to help sensitize you to your informal learning preferences.

Worksheet 1–1. Are You An Informal Learner?

Instructions: Answer these questions. For responses, see the answer key below.

1. One morning when you start your email program, everything looks unfamiliar. You see a notice at the top of the screen: "We've unveiled a new look. Click here to learn more." What do you do first?

   a. Click where indicated to learn more about the changes to the program.
   b. Ask the person in the office next to yours to explain what's going on.
   c. Ignore the invitation to click here and fumble your way through the interface.
   d. Sign up for a class to learn about the new email interface.

2. You're the new coordinator of vendors for your department, which has never used vendors before but plans to start using them in the future. To prepare for this new role, what do you do first?

   a. Ask your friend in the Purchasing Department what to do.
   b. Find the company policies and procedures on managing vendor relationships on the Intranet.
   c. Sign up for a class on managing vendor relationships.
   d. Start the job and figure things out as you go along.

3. Your partner was recently diagnosed with pre-diabetes, and the doctor has urged your partner to adopt a healthier diet. Although you thought you knew what healthy eating was, apparently your daily diet of bran muffin breakfasts and meat-potato-and-salad dinners isn't producing healthy results. To learn about healthy diets, what do you do first?

    a. Continue cooking but remove fat and sugars from the diet.
    b. Join a local diabetes support group.
    c. Register for the "Diabetes Diet" class offered at the hospital.
    d. Visit a website or buy a book with dietary recommendations for pre-diabetes patients.

4. In a meeting this morning, an executive makes several comments related to the company's most recent annual financial report. You're embarrassed to admit this: You don't know how to read a financial report. To correct this problem, what do you do first?

    a. Ask your friend in the Finance Department to give you a crash course in reading financial reports.
    b. Buy *Financial Reports for Dummies* at your nearest bookstore—and read it cover to cover.
    c. Read the report line-for-line and try to glean some meaning from it.
    d. Take the e-learning course, "How to Read a Financial Report," available through the library of e-learning courses in your company.

5. You have accepted the invitation to serve as webmaster for your neighborhood association next year. OK, so you have no experience with webmastering. To prepare for this new role, what do you do first?

    a. Ask the outgoing webmaster to provide step-by-step instructions.
    b. Start your job and figure things out as they arise.
    c. Take an introductory course for webmasters through your local continuing education department.
    d. Watch a series of videos on YouTube about how to be a webmaster.

Scoring

Compute your score using Table 1–A, and interpret your score by checking Table 1–B.

Table 1–A: Scoring the Exercise

Assign Points as Follows	Tally Points Here
1—a-4, b-3, c-2, d-1	_____
2—a-2, b-4, c-1, d-3	_____
3—a-3, b-2, c-1, d-4	_____
4—a-2, b-4, c-3, d-1	_____
5—a-2, b-3, c-1, d-4	_____
Total	_____

Table 1–B: Interpreting Your Score

If You Scored:	You Are:	Which Means That:
5 or below	A formal learner	You generally prefer formal situations for your learning.
6 to 9	A social learner	Although you're able to learn on your own, you often prefer to learn in groups or from other people.
11 to 14	A go-with-the-flow learner	You use a variety of means to learn new skills, sometimes just trying things out to see how well you can perform.
15 to 16	A self-directed informal learner	You develop new skills on your own, but to make sure that you correctly understand them, you frequently refer to outside sources to do so.

With this awareness of your own preferences, you can begin to appreciate the different preferences of other informal learners. Use this awareness to better identify which activities might work with which learners—and which won't—so you can use informal learning to achieve given goals.

2

How Do People Learn Informally?

What's Inside This Chapter

In this chapter, you'll learn

▶ the nine principles of informal learning
▶ the implications of these principles for informal learning in the workplace.

Imagine that your manager told you that, for the next three days, someone else would cover your ongoing responsibilities and you could use the time to explore whatever topic interests you. What would you do?

To figure this out, take a moment now to answer the questions in the activity in Figure 2–1. After you complete the activity, return to this chapter.

Figure 2–1. Consider This: A Hypothetical Opportunity to Pursue Informal Learning in the Workplace

Your manager has given you three days to explore whatever career-related topic that interests you. As you imagine this experience, consider these questions:

1. What topic would you explore? How did you choose the topic?

2. How would you go about researching the topic?

3. What learning activities would you pursue?

4. Would you interact with others? If so, with whom? How?

5. Could you learn accidentally? How?

6. How can you verify whether you accurately learned the content?

7. Given your past personal experiences, what is the likelihood that you will finish your intended program of learning in the three days given to you?

8. How will you remember what you learned?

9. How would you apply the content on the job?

Each of these nine questions considers a different aspect of the process of informal learning. This chapter explores the answers to these questions. The answers synthesize the research on informal learning and, in the process of doing so, offer nine research-based principles regarding it. The chapter closes by suggesting how to incorporate these principles when advocating for informal learning in the workplace.

Nine Principles of Informal Learning

Research has uncovered a number of characteristics about informal learning. Some only show up in a single study; others show up in several. From those characteristics found by many studies, I propose the following principles that training and development professionals should consider when promoting the use of informal learning in their organizations. Note that research on informal learning differs substantially from research on formal learning. To learn a bit about the nature of the research from which these observations emerged, see the sidebar, "About Research on Informal Learning."

Think About This

What is *learning*? To kick off this chapter, we need to establish a common definition of learning so we have a common basis for considering whether learning has occurred. This book defines learning as a purposeful change in behavior resulting from the acquisition of knowledge, skills, and values. The behavior may be a psychomotor (physical) one, but it can also be associated with cognition (intellectual practices) or emotion (values and attitudes).

In addition, this chapter distinguishes between *informal learning* and *true informal learning*:

- *Informal learning* refers to situations in which some combination of the process, location, purpose, and content of instruction is determined by the student, who may or may not be conscious that an instructional event has occurred.

- *True informal learning* refers to situations in which the process, location, purpose, and content of instruction are *all* determined just by the learner, who may or may not be conscious that an instructional event has occurred.

About Research on Informal Learning

Admittedly, research purists looking for "proof" that informal learning works will be disappointed in what they find. They won't find a body of experiments comparing people who studied formally and informally and that show that people who learn informally are just as successful as those who learn formally. Instead they will find other types of evidence. One key source of research on informal learning is surveys of self-reported practices of learning informally. They provide general insights into practices but pose accuracy problems because people often misreport their own practices when answering surveys. Another key source of research on informal learning is qualitative studies, which involves observing workers in real work environments and systematically documenting their informal learning processes, or interviewing workers in-depth to find out how they learned to perform their jobs. These studies generate rich descriptions of the informal learning process, but do not validate the extent to which informal learning actually occurs across organizations, much less the extent to which it "works."

But considered together, these surveys and qualitative studies provide a powerful portrait of informal learning processes in a variety of environments. Furthermore, these studies approach learning from the perspectives of a variety of disciplines, not only adult education, educational technology, and human resource development (the three primary disciplines underlying our work), but also educational psychology, museum studies, technical communication, and even computer science. The growing number of studies and wide variety of environments studied provide a preponderance of evidence about the triumphs and pitfalls that occur during informal learning. The principles presented in this chapter emerge from these types of studies.

Principle 1: Informal Learning Is But One Piece of a Larger Learning Puzzle

Early thinking about informal learning presented it as the opposite of formal learning. For example, representing the view of practicing professionals, informal learning advocate Jay Cross (2007) states that "training is something that's pushed on you; someone else is in charge. Learning is something you choose to do, whether you're being trained or not" and that "formal learning takes place in classrooms; informal learning happens in learnscapes, that is, a learning ecology. It's learning without borders."

Cross shares the early views of researchers Victoria Marsick and Karen Watkins. But over time, Marsick's and Watkins's opinions evolved and they concluded that the two are not separate. Margaret Dale and John Bell (1999) agree, cautioning that "reliance on informal learning alone can lead to drawbacks." Although the processes might not occur on the structured schedule of formal classes, research suggests that many formally prepared resources play a key role in informal learning (Dale and Bell, 1999).

Indeed, research on the transfer of training (such as Burke and Hutchins, 2007; Lim and Morris, 2006) and on electronic performance support systems suggests that informal learning activities can be integrated with formal learning to produce significantly stronger retention of learning than would be feasible through either type of learning alone.

Principle 2: Objectives Play a Different Role in Informal Learning Than in Formal Learning

Early in the process of developing a formal learning program, training and development professionals usually write *instructional objectives*—statements of skills that learners should be able to perform as a result of completing a learning program (Wedman and Tessmer, 1993; Zemke and Lee, 1987). Instructional objectives also identify the conditions under which learners should be able to demonstrate those skills and the level of acceptable performances.

Although concrete, structured objectives serve formal learning programs well, they are often irrelevant to informal learning programs. That's because workers who participate in informal learning efforts prepare their own objectives, whether implicitly or explicitly. The objectives established by workers are of value to them and often do not align with the strategic or operational goals of the employer.

Imposing concrete objectives on informal learning may seem inappropriate because much of the learning is unintentional, unconscious, or both. But write instructional objectives anyway. They can play a pivotal role in managing expectations of the workers who use certain types of published resources for informal learning.

Rather than serving as marching orders that workers must follow, learning objectives help workers determine what the informal learning program covers, so they can assess for themselves whether the program actually meets their needs. Similarly, managers and other experienced people who advise workers can use these objectives to offer meaningful advice about the relevance and value of particular materials and experiences.

In particular, learning objectives that address *psychomotor skills* (ones associated with physical processes) and *cognitive skills* (ones associated with thinking processes) can help workers and advisers determine the appropriateness of a particular learning resource.

Writing *affective* objectives (ones associated with feelings and beliefs) pose a different challenge—and serve a different role in informal learning. Although training and development professionals cannot predict exact changes in beliefs, knowledge, and skills that might result from informal learning, objectives can alert participants to the types of changes that might possibly result.

Informal learning objectives should be more flexible and less concrete than formal learning objectives, alerting potential participants to the possibility of learning and what that learning might address. For example, participants in a professional roundtable of experienced statisticians might "explore answers to vexing questions about statistical analysis." Participants in an affinity group for women might "learn techniques for balancing work and family through interactions with others who face this challenge every day." And participants in a group for summer interns might "support one another with the challenges that arise in the transition from school to work."

Basic Rule

Because informal learning involves unstructured, unconscious, and seren-dipitous learning, three key practices of training and development profes-sionals—writing objectives, offering scheduled learning events, and evaluating programs using the Kirkpatrick methodology—do not apply to informal learning.

Principle 3: Executive and Management Support Strengthens Informal Learning Efforts in the Workplace

This principle addresses the question presented in the activity in Figure 2–1 at the beginning of the chapter: What if you were told that someone would cover your work responsibilities so that you could pursue something that interested you?

My own research with Colleen Bernard has shown that receiving time off work to train is increasingly of concern to workers (Carliner and Bernard, 2011a; Carliner and Bernard, 2011b). We asked participants in our study about their reactions to being told that they would have the opportunity to go to training. We expected responses to reflect participants' perceptions on the value of training, but several surprised us by saying that their first reaction was concern over how they would get their work done. Even during training, employees were still expected to keep up with their usual duties. This finding was consistent with other studies we found, which reported that workers felt guilty about using work time for informal learning (see Westbrook and Veale, 2001).

Perhaps that's the reason for one consistent conclusion of nearly all of the research on informal learning: For it to succeed, workers must feel that they have the support of executives and managers in their learning efforts.

Executive support takes many forms:

▶ providing workers with work time to learn
▶ allowing mistakes to occur throughout the learning process, relieving workers' fears of the repercussions of failing
▶ when feasible, formally recognizing informal learning efforts (Dale and Bell, 1999). (Unconcious learning, of course, is difficult to recognize as workers do not even recognize it themselves.)

But perhaps the most meaningful way that executives and managers can support informal learning is by being informal learners themselves. Margaret Dale and John Bell (1999) specifically suggest that leaders and managers act as role models, and found that workers "observed and copied" their leaders' behavior.

Principle 4: A Variety of Solutions Support Informal Learning

This principle addresses the questions "What learning activities would you pursue?" and "How will you remember what you learned?" from the activity in Figure 2–1.

To get a sense of the types of resources informal learners consult, consider this scenario. You work in the research and development lab of a well-established manufacturer. Your lab follows well-defined design and development processes that the organization has honed during its 50-plus years of existence. Although these processes ensure that all aspects of design and development receive appropriate consideration, and that products receive extensive testing before the company releases them for marketing, it takes your company a minimum of 18 months to complete the design and development of a product. Your competitors are able to complete product design projects in 12 months.

You have heard about a product development process called *agile development*, which lets organizations develop products more quickly and efficiently than traditionally structured development processes. Where do you learn about agile development if you cannot take a formal course on the topic? Several options exist, each with advantages and disadvantages.

▶ Presentations at professional meetings or conferences, or given through webinars. They usually provide a high-level overview of the process but are often presented by advocates, who tend to address the issue at a conceptual level and overemphasize the positive aspects of the methodology and overlook practical issues of implementation.

▶ Articles in professional magazines and on blogs and websites, which often have the same drawbacks as presentations.

▶ Case studies from professional magazines, websites, or conferences, which provide practical insights into the application of the methodology. But most people only publish successful cases that they would like to share with others; few share their failures.

▶ Articles in academic journals that describe the theory underlying the methodology and report the results of research on its application. Although these studies are well constructed, the articles are written by one researcher for another researcher, so the general style and tone of the writing is off-putting, and the link between research and its real-world application is difficult to grasp.

▶ Books on agile technology, which often include general information, case studies, and research—sort of a one-stop shop for all of the content. But books are sometimes costly, either financially or in terms of the amount of time needed to read them.

▶ Discussions with people who have implemented agile processes in their organizations, conducted either in person or through online communities. These provide firsthand opinions and experiences. But people may unintentionally omit essential information.

▶ Experimenting with agile processes on a trial project.

In other words, you have many resources at your disposal to learn about agile methodologies. Each has its advantages and disadvantages and requires a different investment of time, and none provide a complete view of agile processes.

This story illustrates one of the primary challenges of informal learning: Informal learners must rely on several resources to learn about a topic. Promoting informal learning, therefore, involves developing or acquiring a variety of resources, such as published materials, case studies, and activities, as well as offering access to experiences, coaching, and advice that might help workers develop skills on their own—and building comfort among managers and workers for this multipart approach.

Often, designing and developing some of these resources is challenging because doing so involves capturing and reporting *tacit content*—ideas, plans, guidelines, and approaches that are undocumented yet exist in the heads of workers. In contrast, *explicit* content is formally documented, such as organizational structures and responsibilities, processes, work standards, product plans, and job descriptions. Intellectual capital authors Leif Edvisson and Michael Malone (1997) characterize tacit content as all of the material that leaves the building when people leave work and explicit content as all of the material that stays.

In many cases, these explicit resources can support learning, even though they were not designed specifically for training workers. Training and development professionals need to make workers and managers aware that these resources exist and encourage them to consult as many as possible. Here are some specific issues that training and development professionals need to address when promoting the use of existing resources for informal learning:

- regularly reminding workers and managers about the availability of the materials
- helping workers locate all of this information and critically assess its relevance, accuracy, and *balance* (that is, assess whether the materials present one or more points of view)
- encouraging workers not only to rely on published or formally presented content, but also to actively discuss topics with others who have insights to share
- providing workers with repeated exposure to the topic
- encouraging workers to seek out experiences such as pilot projects and developmental assignments that provide opportunities to apply skills
- reminding workers that the most complete learning comes from engagement with several sources, rather than relying solely on one.

Basic Rule

Learning informally is a journey that shapes knowledge, attitudes, beliefs, and skills through ongoing interactions with a variety of resources and experiences. The journey often lacks a map; rather, each interaction deepens understanding and refines the path of the journey.

Principle 5: Left on Their Own, Informal Learners Follow Their Own Paths

Studies of the ways people learn from museum exhibits provide insights into the ways people learn informally. Researchers John Falk and Lynn Dierking (2000) asked visitors to a natural history museum what they learned immediately after the visit—and followed up with them a few times in the subsequent months. Falk and Dierking noted that the visitors tended to choose exhibitions related to subjects they already knew a lot about and that they retained something of what they learned during their visit. Visitors who had a higher level of interest to begin with retained more.

Such findings are consistent with the Knowles' principles of adult learning (Knowles, Swanson, and Holton, 2011), which state that adult learners prefer relevant material that they can apply in their lives.

These findings also suggest that informal learners tend to explore topics of high interest to themselves and only nominally explore topics of interest to others. This means that, left completely to their own devices, informal learners are most likely to explore what interests them, which may or may not serve the learning agenda the organization would like to establish.

In the absence of internal motivation to learn, research has also shown that external incentives can sometimes motivate workers to take informal and self-directed learning more seriously. Sometimes the incentives are explicit. For example, an early study of e-learning found that completion rates for courses with a tangible outcome, such as a certification, or that employers required, such as compliance training, resulted in higher completion rates than those with open outcomes, such as improving proficiency with a spreadsheet or authoring tool.

Other times incentives are internal and implicit, such as when workers choose to learn to solve an immediate problem they face (Marsick, 2009). Sveinung Skule (2004) adds that, if a job demands learning, workers tend to take the initiative. At the least, they do so to ensure that they continue to perform satisfactorily in their jobs.

Whatever the incentive to learn, ideally the informal learning agendas of workers and employers would align. But a complete alignment of goals is not realistic. For example, some communication researchers have expressed concern that, when people explore topics on their own, they often seek to validate their own positions. People might even read material with opposing views but do so to reinforce and validate their own views.

Furthermore, Margaret Dale and John Bell (1999) found that informal learning can be so narrowly focused that workers might only learn part of a task, or learn so superficially that they cannot transfer their learning to other situations: a goal that most managers have for learning. For example, a worker might learn how to present interactive television courses but not transfer those skills to the virtual classroom (which has many of the characteristics of interactive television).

In other cases, informal learning can generate unwanted tension. Consider the worker in a software development group studying *open source software*, a type of software in which the software publishers make the programming instructions available for free, with the expectation that users will improve and extend the capabilities of that software. But the software project on which he was working was well under way using proprietary software, in which the programming is not available for free, and users are not allowed to make changes to the software. Scrapping the proprietary software already developed, as the worker recommended, would be expensive, but failing to do so in this market could ultimately prove even more costly, if users are already showing a preference for open source software. In other words, informal learning raised change management issues (in this case, a change of course for product development). Formal learning raises the same issues, but those changes are initiated from the top down—changes that the leadership of the organization has already chosen to embrace but for which workers might not yet be ready. In informal learning, the proposed changes cause similar discomfort, but from the bottom up.

Two other practical issues arise from learners following their own paths. Research suggests that experienced workers engage in informal learning at high rates, sometimes as their primary means of skill development. In fact, many studies that look at participation in training suggest that the more experienced the workers, the less likely they will participate in formal training. But informal training alone might not be sufficient to keep skills current.

Additionally, as this conversation has implied, informal learning happens on its own schedule. That is, workers learn when they need to—and at a pace that suits them. In some workplaces, that's often not fast enough. If time to performance is an issue, then *true* informal learning might not be in an organization's best interest.

Principle 6: Many Informal Learners Have an Incomplete Tool Kit of Learning Techniques

This principle addresses the questions "How would you go about researching the topic?" and "Given your own past personal experience, what is the likelihood that you will finish your intended program of learning in the three days given to you?" from the activity in Figure 2–1.

Although the Internet makes large volumes of information available to readers, research suggests that many informal learners have limited skills at vetting the information they encounter (Bennett, Maton, and Kervin, 2008). For example, in a case study of a technical support group, Joe Downing (2006) found that workers don't use appropriate search terms—resulting in too little or too much information. The customer support representatives in this case also relied too heavily on the first items in the search results without assessing the quality of the information found. This led to the workers offering incomplete or incorrect information to callers.

This case illustrates some of the challenges inherent in informal learning. The first is figuring out whether workers learned the material "correctly." Many informal learners lack the tools to do this. To be fair, learners have often learned one core lesson correctly but often lack other essential pieces of information. In the case of the technical support group, the workers knew they had to find answers quickly because callers were waiting. But they confused the first responses to their searches with accurate answers.

A second challenge lies in overcoming prior knowledge and beliefs. Researcher Richard Clark (2010) notes that, although un-learning old knowledge is possible, it's not necessarily easy because—as researcher Mary Cseh (1998) noted—existing mental models often guide thinking.

A third challenge is determining actual completion of an informal learning program. This is difficult to pin down because, in *true* informal learning, completion occurs when workers decide for themselves that they've finished. That usually occurs when workers feel they have achieved their learning goal, even if they have not formally finished the learning activity (such as a self-study course or a user's guide). Sometimes that sense of completion occurs within minutes of starting a program. Perhaps this explains why many organizations report that many workers do not complete e-learning courses.

Further complicating the issue of completion is the fact that informal learning rarely occurs through a formally scheduled event. It happens by checking a webpage here, a user's guide there, and a similar compilation of experiences and resources. Such learning has no official beginning, so it follows that it has no official end.

What both experience and research suggest is that, when considering the use of informal learning, training and development professionals and their organizations must address workers' abilities to

- ▶ efficiently locate information
- ▶ assess the quality of the information
- ▶ recognize when prior learning interferes with new learning
- ▶ distinguish between significant and insignificant learning issues.

Training and development professionals must also assess whether workers have learned the material correctly, and find out what would motivate workers to finish their informal learning effort, especially if it is externally motivated.

Addressing these issues requires that organizations provide support for informal learning. To some extent, supporting a natural and unconscious process admittedly sounds like an oxymoron. But as described in chapter 1, informal learning has varying levels of consciousness and formality—and organizations can match the level of support with the level of formality of the program. Chapter 4 explores in depth how organizations can support informal learning.

Think About This

Although informal learning is a journey on which many workers embark on their own, that journey need not be a solitary one. The challenge for training and development professionals is to figure out ways to guide workers on these learning journeys and provide them with the resources they need to make good progress on them.

Principle 7: Informal Learning Is Often a Social Activity

This principle addresses the question "Would you interact with others? If so, with whom? How?" from the activity in Figure 2–1.

In their research, Marilyn Laiken, Karen Edge, Stephen Friedman, and Karima West (2008) found that much learning occurs through collaboration on work teams. They found that learning occurred as co-workers finished assignments, participated in meetings, and discussed issues with colleagues both formally through meetings and informally through chance encounters in the workplace.

Workers also rely on people beyond their immediate work environment for learning. Sinan Aral (2010), among other researchers, has explored the role of networks: who knows whom, who interacts with whom, who influences whom, and how ideas flow through networks to gain credibility and acceptance. These networks often involve people in and out of the immediate work environment—and inside and outside of the organization—and are valuable sources of news, technical content, advice, and insights. Workers who have questions about a particular issue and have access to an expert on that issue through their personal network may be able to receive quick answers. This saves not only time but also money, because the expert usually does not charge for a quick reply to an email inquiry.

Mentoring, participation in professional and community associations, contacts made through blogging and publishing, and networks of former co-workers and classmates all contribute to the development of networks that can be tapped.

Most employers embrace networking within their organizations, because they believe it leads to efficiencies and breaks down barriers between departments, divisions, and locations. Chapter 5 explores specific types of informal learning that leverage groups and social interactions.

Principle 8: Evaluating Informal Learning Challenges Existing Evaluation Methodologies

This principle addresses the question "How can you verify whether you accurately learned the content?" from the activity in Figure 2–1.

To get a sense of the challenges of evaluating informal learning, consider what you would do if your manager asked you to provide a report on the effectiveness of informal learning in your organization. If you have received formal training in training and development, your first temptation might be to follow Kirkpatrick's four-level methodology and attempt to calculate the return-on-investment (ROI).

To evaluate the first level—reaction—you might attempt to assess satisfaction with the learning event. But, as noted earlier, a complete informal learning program often involves several learning resources. Some lend themselves easily to the evaluation of reactions, such as self-study programs like online tutorials and formally scheduled events like lunch-and-learn sessions. Others, such as informal conversations with co-workers and similar impromptu activities, are not so easily evaluated.

Similarly, to evaluate the second level—learning—you might be tempted to develop a test to assess the extent to which workers have mastered the learning objectives or a rubric so you can observe how well workers apply their newly developed competencies.

Tests and observations might work for a self-study course or a well-defined on-the-job training program, but how would you assess other types of informal learning? In *true* informal learning, workers establish their own objectives, and often not in measurable terms.

These issues with objectives complicate Level 3 (transfer of behavior) and Level 4 (impact) evaluations. Without objectives, training and development professionals lack a basis for evaluation.

These examples demonstrate that traditional evaluation based on Kirkpatrick's four levels falls flat. Kirkpatrick's framework assumes that learning happens in formally defined events that have well-defined objectives and are intended to address a business need. None of these necessarily apply to informal learning, even informal learning for the workplace.

Much of informal learning results from a process in which several experiences—some planned, many unplanned—result in changes in behavior, knowledge, beliefs, or attitudes. Some of the changes are visible and easily identified; others are unconscious and require extensive work to uncover. Chapter 8 explores in more detail a different tool kit to identify what workers learned through informal learning and the extent of that learning.

Principle 9: The Nature of Informal Learning Substantially Differs From That of Formal Learning

This principle addresses the question "How would you apply the content on the job?" from the activity in Figure 2–1.

As suggested earlier, formal learning begins with well-defined and measurable objectives and is deemed successful when evaluations show that those objectives have been achieved. For example, a person taking a project management certificate course might only be deemed successful if he or she passes the certification examination.

In contrast, informal learning often begins with fuzzy goals and is deemed successful when workers themselves feel that they have benefitted from the learning.

These goals have extensive flexibility. What starts out as a search for job enrichment can accidentally result in a new job or career. For example, a programmer might teach a one-time class for her co-workers and have such a positive experience that she decides to become a full-time training and development professional.

Outcomes can be tangible, like new jobs and different work assignments, but they can also be intangible, such as the confidence that comes with knowledge and experience. Consider again the programmer who decides to become a training and development professional. As a result of regularly reading the magazine *Psychology Today* for her own interest, she already has a strong foundation in learning processes.

The tight definitions of formal learning and the more flexible approaches of informal learning are rooted in different philosophies of learning—that is, different beliefs about the nature of knowledge and knowing. Formal learning in a training context is primarily rooted in a philosophy called *behaviorism*, which defines learning as a change in behavior. Fundamentally, behaviorism is based on a belief that knowledge is fixed and is consistent across individuals. This is why formal learning programs are designed in a way that allows us to identify and measure behaviors that change as a result of the learning.

In contrast, informal learning is rooted in a philosophy called *constructivism*, which characterizes learning not as a change in behavior but as a change in knowledge, beliefs, and attitudes—many of which cannot be observed or measured, and some of which are reflected in new skills and processes.

Constructivism suggests that knowledge is built (constructed) through experience and influenced by interactions with people. As a result, the knowledge base of each person differs because each person has a unique body of experience and knowledge. Informal learning reflects this philosophy. It often begins with flexible goals that are assessed afterward to find out how the learning experience affected the worker.

Although constructivist learning can occur in a formal class setting, it actually happens wherever people encounter new knowledge, beliefs, and attitudes. As a result, constructivism often portrays learning as a journey or process rather than an event.

This difference in philosophies between formal and informal learning, especially *true* informal learning, explains why so many of the core practices of training and development professionals, such as writing objectives, offering courses, and conducting tests and transfer evaluations, do not neatly transfer to informal learning. Those practices are rooted in a different value system.

The lack of written objectives, formal courses, and evaluation, however, could raise issues with stakeholders who expect more traditional measures of the reach and impact of learning programs. Chapter 4 suggests some ways to manage expectations regarding these issues and offers some encouraging news from the research about the flexibility of stakeholders. Chapter 8 suggests some ways that training and development professionals can provide stakeholders with meaningful data about the reach and impact of informal learning programs.

Incorporating These Principles When Advocating for Informal Learning in the Workplace

The approaches presented in this chapter provide a framework for applying informal learning to a broad range of challenges, from structured experiences that orient new employees to their jobs to loosely defined but essential experiences for developing prospective leaders. Because the formality varies among these learning experiences, each requires a similarly flexible approach to support and evaluation.

But specifically when and how can you apply informal learning? The next chapter addresses that question, by suggesting specific instances over the life cycle of a job in which workers can use informal learning to strengthen their knowledge and skills and nurture their careers.

Getting It Done

The following section helps you integrate the principles of informal learning by helping you consider ways you use informal learning resources in your daily life, both inside and outside the workplace.

First, consider how to apply the principles of informal learning in your daily life by trying the activity in Worksheet 2–1. Second, consider informal learning in the context of your job. Try the exercise in Worksheet 2–2 to find out ways that informal learning affects your work and the manner in which the principles described apply to your work environment.

Worksheet 2–1. Clarifying Informal Learning Processes

How do informal learning processes work? Try this exercise to find out.

Imagine that someone has asked you to share five tips about shopping. Share those tips now.

_____

_____

_____

_____

_____

Now, identify how you learned each of these tips.

_____

_____

_____

_____

_____

Debriefing. Did you learn any of those tips in a class? If you're like most of the people with whom I have tested this activity, the answer is no. Most of us do not go to shopping class. Instead, we learn about shopping through experience. Table 2–1 presents examples of tips that people have shared over the years and how they learned them.

Table 2–1. Examples of Shopping Tips Learned Through Informal Learning

Tip	How the Person Learned It
Don't take your teenaged children with you to the grocery store; they tend to run up the bill with impulse purchases.	A nagging sense that the bill was higher, confirmed by comparing receipts of visits with and without the teenagers
You can keep electronic coupons on your smartphone; you do not need to print them.	Cashier at the pet store

Tip	How the Person Learned It
If you do not use your Groupon (or similar) offer, contact the store anyway. They often will honor the face value of the Groupon. For example, if you paid $50 for $100 in food and drink at a restaurant and did not use the Groupon before the expiration, the merchant might honor the $50 credit.	Calling the restaurant
If you do not have a promotion code for an item you buy online, search for one before buying.	Conversation with a friend
AAA/CAA rates at most hotels rival the advance purchase rates, but—unlike advance purchase rates—let you change or cancel your reservation without penalty until 6 p.m. on the day of the reservation.	Reviewing the terms and conditions of the rates on hotel websites

Worksheet 2–2. Clarifying Informal Learning Processes in a Work-Related Context

List five things that you learned accidentally on the job.

_____

_____

_____

_____

_____

For each thing you listed above, identify how you learned it.

_____

_____

_____

_____

_____

Now, determine for each whether the thing you learned was something that should have been learned formally or informally.

_____

_____

_____

_____

_____

Debriefing. If your experiences are like those of people who have tried this exercise before, your list will include this type of information:

- Policies and procedures, often learned either in passing or when the learner violated a previously unknown rule.
- Tips for using software more effectively and efficiently. These tips commonly involve keyboard shortcuts and increased efficiency with the software. People say that they learn these tips in a variety of ways: from co-workers, articles, and presentations.
- Tips for designing and facilitating instructional programs. For example, one instructional designer learned to list items on multiple-choice questions in alphabetical order from a presentation at a conference. An instructor learned to use a particular type of clapping to end exercises by observing another instructor using that technique in a workshop.

How to Use Formal and Informal Learning in the Workplace

What's Inside This Chapter

In this chapter, you'll learn

▶ the learning needs of workers at specific phases, or *touchpoints*, in the tenures of their jobs

▶ how combinations of formal and informal learning can address those needs.

The last two chapters explored what informal learning is and the principles guiding the process of learning informally. But how do you actually integrate informal learning into an ongoing program for developing the skills and knowledge of workers in your organization?

To help you consider this, think about the five individuals introduced in chapter 1:

▶ Casey, who's just started her job as an assistant manager at a clothing store in the mall

▶ Ricardo, the customer service agent who works in the auto call center for a major insurance company

▶ Curtis, the site supervisor for a construction firm who misunderstood his company's human resources policies

▶ Marley, the junior account executive with an advertising agency who was mentored to success

▶ Karin, the systems engineer for a software company who found a unique way to solve a computer software issue.

These individuals hold different jobs, are at different points in their careers, and face different job-related challenges and, as a result, have different learning needs.

This chapter suggests a framework you can use to address the learning needs of such a diverse group of workers. The framework identifies key phases, called *touch-points,* during the life cycle of a job that generate specific needs for learning in the context of the job. This chapter describes those needs, and the combinations of formal and informal learning activities that can support workers at any given phase. Examples based on the five workers just described illustrate how to transfer these concepts to your own workplace.

Matching Formal and Informal Learning Opportunities With Learning Needs

Training and development professionals typically take a content-based approach to their work: They identify the general technical skills and knowledge needed in a particular job, then produce appropriate training materials.

This approach primarily addresses what workers *do*. But it often overlooks the reality that the longer workers stay in their jobs, the more the jobs become tailored to the unique talents and interests of those workers. As noted earlier in this book, informal learning excels at helping workers form attitudes and personalize knowledge and skills to their own particular situations.

For example, because she is new to her position and has limited knowledge of it, Casey needs structured learning to master the technical aspects of her job. But she also needs an introduction to the organization. Although most onboarding programs cover the history and values of the organization, "introduction to the organization" onboarding also helps new workers develop a sense of belonging to their organizations. In her job as a systems engineer, Karin addresses issues that no one has anticipated and for which no clear answer exists. She must creatively devise a solution, be prepared to fail, and if she does fail, try alternatives until she solves the problem.

Research has demonstrated such differences in learning needs over the life of a job. In a study of the ways that people develop expertise in their professions, researcher Michael Eraut (2000) found that the nature of the problems workers encounter changes the longer workers stay in their jobs. Early in their tenures, workers focus on determining which types of problems they need to solve, a process called *pattern recognition*. As workers become more experienced, the focus changes to understanding the broader situation in which they are working, a process called *meta-cognition*.

Research like this suggests that the life cycle of the job provides a framework that training and development professionals can use to anticipate the changing learning needs of workers throughout their job life cycles. *Life cycle* refers to the span of a worker's tenure in a given position, from the time the worker starts the job until he or she moves on to the next position or leaves the organization. During this life cycle, workers' problem-solving strategies transition from pattern recognition to meta-cognition.

Throughout the life cycle, workers must also address ongoing organizational initiatives such as change management programs, quality improvement initiatives, and revisions to policies, work standards, products, and processes. Figure 3–1 identifies the key junctures during the life cycle of a job.

Each of these junctures, or phases, in the life cycle of a job presents opportunities for learning. In most phases, external factors drive the learning process, such as a request by a manager for a worker to assume additional responsibilities, switching to new software programs, or a changing procedure or policy. In many of these instances, employers often provide little formal training so workers have to figure out for themselves how to address these requests.

The following sections explore learning at each touchpoint in depth. Each describes learning goals typical of that touchpoint. Then each section explains how workers typically initiate and follow through on the learning process, how employers

Figure 3–1. Opportunities for Learning During the Life Cycle of a Job

Orient workers to the technical aspects of a job.	Onboard workers to the culture and values of the group.	Expand the scope of assignments a worker can handle.	Build workers' proficiency.	Help workers address undocumented challenges.	Update workers' skills and knowledge.	Help workers choose career goals.	Prepare workers for their next jobs.
		Address ongoing organizational initiatives.					
New to the job							Ready to graduate to the next job

and workers participate in setting the agenda needed to master the learning goals, and how training and development professionals can support workers in integrating the content learned into their jobs.

Basic Rule
The different phases in the life cycle of a job shape both the need for learning and the nature of it.

Touchpoint 1: Orienting Workers to the Technical Aspects of a Job

Consider the situation of the new assistant manager, Casey. As she starts her job, her manager's first concern is teaching Casey how to perform it according to the standards of the organization. Casey needs to learn how to follow the designated work processes using the designated resources, such as particular software and computers. In Casey's situation, that means she needs to learn about the products stocked in a store, how to use the point of sale system (the technical term for cash register), and standard procedures she will oversee, such as opening and closing the store and processing returns.

This process of learning how to perform a new job is called *orientation*. Orientation needs to introduce workers to the processes, procedures, deliverables, standards of quality, and policies that guide the work, as well as to related terminology and concepts. Because employers have a strong idea of the performance they seek from new workers, they primarily take the lead in setting the learning agenda and structuring the experience for orientation.

Because a typical department in an organization has five to 15 workers and usually hires just one or two workers at a time, most organizations cannot offer new workers a formally scheduled orientation course. So by necessity, at least some of this orientation happens informally even in the largest organizations, usually through structured self-directed learning.

In these structured self-study orientations, new workers typically receive a tour of the work area, and a manager or senior worker introduces the new worker to the staff of the department. The new worker also receives materials to read (sometimes in print, but increasingly online) and may take some self-study courses on general technical topics, such as safety issues and overviews of processes followed by several departments.

Although new workers typically have high levels of motivation when they start a new job, they usually have limited knowledge about their specific jobs and limited confidence in their abilities to perform them. As a result, even if the learning occurs informally on the job, workers benefit from a high level of support and structure at this phase of learning, especially in the first days and weeks. Such structure not only ensures that workers have covered and mastered the key material, but also provides workers with feedback on their on-the-job performance (even after formal training has ended) so they can build appropriate skills and confidence in their abilities to perform.

Even if they do not prepare formal learning programs for this phase of development, training and development professionals can support orientation efforts by preparing general self-study materials that apply to all jobs, templates (similar to fill-in-the-blank forms) that departments can use to structure their orientation efforts, and checklists and discussion guides to coach managers and senior workers who oversee the orientation process.

Think About This

Although the learning goals might be externally driven and well-established external criteria for completion exist, informal methods can help new workers acquire skills and knowledge and integrate this material into their work.

Touchpoint 2: Onboarding Workers to the Culture and Values of the Group

Let's return to Casey. In addition to learning how to perform her job, she also needs to be integrated into her immediate work team—the staff of the store—as well as the company with which her store is associated. So besides orienting her to the tasks of her job, her employer needs to *onboard* Casey into the organization: that is, introduce her to the culture and values of the group so that she understands them, models the values for her staff, and can successfully navigate the organizational structure.

As with orientation, the extent of onboarding needed varies among individuals. Workers starting their first jobs, interns, and co-ops (students working in cooperative education programs, in which they combine work and school) often need onboarding to both the organization and the more basic culture of work, such as what to wear, how to speak, and how to interact with others. These basic skills are called *foundational competencies* in the ASTD Competency Model. Other terms include *essential skills* and *workplace literacy*. Many younger workers do not have role models for these skills or the opportunities to develop them; therefore, they must learn these skills.

But most workers are not starting their first jobs; they're just starting new jobs. Many of these workers are new to their organizations and need to be integrated. That integration involves forging cordial relationships with co-workers and determining how the new culture is similar to, and differs from, that of the previous employer. Some differences might be obvious, but others will be subtle, and workers may not notice them for quite some time.

Other new workers receive their jobs through internal transfers. Although they likely need little if any socialization into the organization as a whole, these workers do need to reorient their perspectives to the new department, and to forge relationships with their new co-workers.

Although the facts and language of a culture can be taught, ultimately, most people integrate into a culture by interacting with it. Most organizations use a variety of formal and informal approaches to integrate workers, including lunches and coffee breaks with managers, co-workers, and affinity groups, as well as mentoring.

Some organizations also use e-learning to introduce workers to the history, structure, key products and services, and internal terminology of the organization. But training and development professionals need to be careful about how they present this material to workers: Although e-learning is useful for presenting factual information, sitting workers in front of a computer to learn all about how the company believes "people are our most valuable asset" contradicts the message.

Touchpoint 3: Expanding the Scope of Assignments a Worker Can Handle

Once new workers have successfully mastered the basics of a job and integrated into their organizations, they soon reach a point at which they can expand the scope of assignments they can handle. For example, after new employee orientation, a new assistant store manager like Casey might be able to assist customers, operate the cash register and override problems that arise during the checkout or return process, and open and close the store. But as she masters these tasks, Casey can take on additional responsibilities, such as preparing work schedules and overseeing the stocking of merchandise on the sales floor.

Expanding the scope of assignments workers can handle is the third touchpoint for learning over the life cycle of a job. In general, learning goals at this touchpoint revolve around the following:

- ▶ expanding the scope of responsibilities that a new worker can autonomously handle
- ▶ providing "stretch" opportunities—that is, chances to build skills beyond those the worker uses in the current job.

Mastering some of the additional job responsibilities involves performing well-defined tasks, just like those taught in the technical orientation to the job. But many of these expanded responsibilities involve judgment, such as whether to allow a customer to receive a refund, whether a part delivered by a supplier meets specifications, and which of three programming instructions might work most effectively in a particular situation. Most of these responsibilities also require some prerequisite knowledge and on-the-job experience. This shift from performing well-defined tasks to making judgment calls marks the beginning of the transition from problem-solving strategies that rely on pattern matching to ones that rely on meta-cognition. Before employers trust such responsibilities to newer workers, they need to feel comfortable that these workers can handle these additional responsibilities.

Most workers learn how to take on these new assignments and responsibilities informally on the job, through methods such as casual conversations, follow-up one-on-one coaching, and reading the documentation of processes, policies, procedures, and techniques in guides, operations manuals, references, and job aids.

Both the worker and the organization participate in setting the agenda for learning how to expand the scope of assignments. Sometimes the worker initiates the request for learning; other times a manager suggests a learning opportunity to a worker.

The level of structure needed to master the learning varies, depending on the exact nature of the new responsibilities, the type of content to be learned, and the environment in which the learning is applied. In the least structured situations, like learning to use a software application to perform advanced tasks, workers might learn on their own and apply the learning with little support and without much need for recognition.

In some moderately structured situations, workers might need to perform tasks in a particular way, but only receive feedback as part of an ongoing work process. If they need guidance in applying the learning, the process builds in that guidance. For example, a technical writer who is documenting a more complex product as part of her expanded job responsibilities receives feedback on her work as part of the review process that always follows the writing of a draft.

In the most structured situations, employers might need to verify that workers have properly learned and adapted the content before using it on the job. This usually occurs in work contexts in which liability and safety play central roles, such as in the healthcare industry, or in which consistency of service is essential, such in as the hospitality industry.

Touchpoint 4: Building Workers' Proficiency

Ricardo, the customer service agent whose specialty is directing customers to the auto repair shops in their areas that have the strongest customer satisfaction records, did not develop this special expertise overnight. From his first day on the job, Ricardo fielded calls from every part of the country and needed to provide information about repair shops in communities about which he knew little or nothing. Always a good conversationalist, however, Ricardo casually noted customers' experiences with different repair shops and later learned, by accident, about internal databases that provide information on the quality of work provided by different repair shops. Ricardo realized that by applying this knowledge, he could provide a higher level of service to his customers.

In learning how to recommend the best auto repair shops, Ricardo expanded his repertoire of skills and in the process became a more productive, valuable worker. Building such proficiency is the next touchpoint in the life cycle of a worker in a job. The employer may initiate the learning at this stage, or employees themselves may do so, as Ricardo did. Frequently, learning at this phase happens unconsciously or unintentionally, as happened with Ricardo.

Workers trying to build their proficiency in a job use many of the same learning methods used to help workers expand the scopes of their assignments. Some of the learning might occur through formal programs (some intended primarily for learning, some not), such as online tutorials, workbooks, webinars, presentations, and short classes. But the majority of it happens on the job, especially through interactions with co-workers, coaching, self-study, trial-and-error, and by observing recurring patterns in their work. Because the types of opportunities to learn vary widely at this phase, so does the level of structure needed to learn.

Some workers might need help recognizing that opportunities for greater proficiency exist. Part of that results from a tendency of some to overrate their skill levels. Believing they are already proficient, they might dismiss the idea that there is any room for improvement. But even if they do not overrate their skills, workers might not realize that greater proficiency is possible. Other workers are open to building their proficiency, but have difficulty synthesizing ideas and insights learned through conversations and work experiences into skills they can use on the job.

Touchpoint 5: Helping Workers Address Undocumented Challenges

Karin, the systems engineer for a software company, helps clients customize their software and troubleshoot problems that customers cannot solve on their own, and for which no formal written instructions exist.

Workers who address undocumented challenges often have the highest levels of expertise in their work, and most develop that level of expertise—the fifth touchpoint—through the following ways:

- ▶ refining problem-solving strategies, especially strategies for diagnosing problems and manipulating software and hardware, or similarly complex work equipment, to accomplish the intended goals
- ▶ reading and listening to cases of challenges that others have successfully and unsuccessfully addressed
- ▶ seeking the advice of others who have complementary expertise
- ▶ trial and error in their own work assignments, followed by reflection (whether conscious or not).

Some research suggests that these workers find case studies especially valuable in solving undocumented challenges. Although the cases are rarely identical to the challenges these workers want to address, they are often similar, and workers can determine which aspects of a case apply in their situation. The cases take a variety of forms: case studies (whether formally published or informally shared in conversation), articles, presentations, reports, and simulation exercises.

Workers can learn the general strategies for solving problems through formal and informal learning. Formal learning tends to speed up the learning process and can ensure that workers follow prescribed problem-solving strategies, if the organization prefers that. Simulation speeds the learning process further because, in addition to preparing workers for worst-case scenarios in "safe" learning environments, simulation can present workers with a variety of vexing situations that they might not readily encounter on the job but that are central to building expertise.

But many experts are self-taught in solving problems in their areas of expertise, using strategies learned through reading, watching others, and trial and error. Nearly all experts who handle undocumented problems have honed their expertise and expanded the range of challenges they can comfortably address through informal learning.

Unless the organization transfers the worker to a different project (and, therefore, requires that the worker develop expertise in a completely different subject), workers dealing with undocumented challenges typically establish their own goals for learning. They usually have the motivation to initiate and complete learning, as well as the self-awareness to determine whether they have learned applicable content. That said, even expert workers can make mistakes in their learning process, so access to someone who can assist them in validating choices is helpful. Also, because much of what workers need to learn is not documented, success in learning depends on workers' abilities to tap the tacit knowledge of other experts. Therefore, both networks and interpersonal skills become important to successful informal learning in this development phase.

Think About This

As workers progress further in the life cycles of their jobs, learning goals move from mastering known content and well-defined skills to addressing increasingly original challenges, for which few, if any, documented processes and defined skills exist. This poses limitations to defining learning objectives and outcomes. So learning goals at these later touchpoints are increasingly characterized by loosely defined objectives, self-defined measures of success, and learning through experience—some of the key characteristics of *true* informal learning.

Touchpoint 6: Updating Workers' Skills

Consider again both Ricardo, the customer service representative in a home and auto insurance call center, and Karin, the systems engineer. Both work in fast-changing industries. For example, the insurance industry faces new regulations each year that affect what companies can charge, whom they must cover, what they can cover, and consumers' rights to information and services. Even without changes in regulations, insurance companies regularly introduce new types of policies and update the computer systems used to track customers. This means that Ricardo needs to keep up with the changes in the insurance industry, his company, its products and services, the processes used to interact with customers, and systems used to track those interactions to make sure that he provides customers with the correct information about his company—and gives his company correct information about its customers and prospects.

Meanwhile, Karin's company faces stiff competition, so it launches new products every two to three months, some of which incorporate new technologies that Karin has not encountered before. To make sure she can knowledgeably answer questions posed to her by customers and internal staff, Karin must keep current with product developments.

Keeping up-to-date on changes within a worker's company and industry, its products, work tools, processes, policies, and procedures is the next touchpoint in the life cycle of a job and the primary learning goal at this phase. Changes launched by an organization or arising in the work context drive learning needs at this phase and affect workers at all phases in the tenures of their jobs. Specifically, workers must keep abreast of these types of changes:

▸ updates to products and services and information about their target markets
▸ new versions of software and comparisons with the older versions
▸ announcements about new and changed policies and procedures
▸ general updates on the industry and technologies central to their organization's technical content.

Challenges to learning at this phase involve figuring out what workers need to learn and communicating it in such a way that they cannot miss the message. For substantive changes, most organizations rely on formal change management plans to support learning processes. For incremental changes (which comprise the majority of content that workers must master in this phase), learning usually occurs informally, often through reading information about the change.

Training and development professionals can use several approaches to help workers update their skills, including:

- Personalized news services that compile news about a particular topic from a variety of sources into a single news "feed." Really Simple Syndication (RSS) serves a similar purpose by providing updates from websites of interest to a worker.
- Briefing meetings that provide a targeted audience with a summary of developments in areas of interest to them. These briefings may occur face-to-face, through webcasts, or through video or audio recordings.
- Press releases and news reports about individual changes. These may appear in internal newsletters, trade journals and reports, or the popular press.
- Guided tours, which are short video presentations that provide viewers with an overview of the changes and how the changes might affect everyday tasks.

The level of support that learners need to master a change varies. For changes in occupational or professional knowledge—such as the knowledge needed by a physical therapist or an accountant—workers typically have primary responsibility for initiating the learning. For example, licensed electrical engineers are expected to keep up with developments in their field on their own, with little or no prodding from their employers. For changes in organizational knowledge—such as new products, services, policies, and procedures—the organization has the primary responsibility for initiating learning. To make sure that workers maintain current knowledge, however, many employers include this requirement in the performance plans of their workers.

Touchpoint 7: Helping Workers Choose Career Goals

Ricardo has worked in the call center of an insurance company for six years, rising to the level of senior customer service representative. But his current position offers no more opportunities for advancement, and Ricardo has at least 30 years before he is eligible for retirement. So both Ricardo and his manager are thinking about his next job.

Choosing the next career step is the next phase in the life cycle of a job. In some instances, workers reach this touchpoint because they have, like Ricardo, outgrown their jobs. In other cases, workers reach this touchpoint because their jobs have become obsolete.

Because it focuses on decision making, the primary goal of this touchpoint is development rather than learning. Workers devise plans for their future after considering their needs, interests, capabilities, and the options available. Learning occurs in the process of clarifying interests and needs, validating options, and determining next steps. For many workers, clarifying interests poses quite the challenge. Such clarifications might involve consideration of new and possibly unfamiliar career paths.

Several developmental activities help workers clarify their interests, including career assessments and process portfolios. The results of these activities inform workers about career possibilities and, ideally, provide a list of qualifications they have—and those they need—to enter those careers.

In addition to clarifying interests, workers also need to identify needs that can expand or limit career options: preferred geographical location, family considerations, hobbies and interests, the lifestyle to which the worker aspires (and the income needed to support it), and requirements for the occupations under consideration, such as additional education and scheduling. Workers can address these issues on their own, but they may benefit from some coaching at this phase. For example, if Ricardo needs to remain in his community, he needs to decline a new career that requires a move to another place.

After identifying their interests and clarifying their needs, workers need to validate their options. Informational interviews, job shadowing, and short internships provide workers with some firsthand experience of their options.

Also, having a knowledgeable coach who can, at the least, provide complete factual information and, at the most, serve as a sounding board helps workers make informed decisions about their futures.

This touchpoint closes with workers choosing their next career moves. In some cases, workers handle this choice informally. In other cases, they do so formally through the career development planning processes that many organizations use. Formal career planning provides a structure for thinking about all of the issues that a worker needs to consider when planning for his or her next career. Figure 3–2 shows a sample career development form.

In organizations that require workers to participate in career planning, the employer nominally initiates the process. More frequently, workers initiate career planning when they feel motivated to move to the next stages of their careers or when employers feel that workers are ready to "graduate" from their current positions. When workers initiate the process, they may or may not share that news with their employers.

Figure 3–2. Generic Template for a Career Development Plan

Long-term plan: State the worker's short- (one-year), medium- (two- to five-year), and long-term (five- to 10-year) plans. Specifically state where the worker would like to go during those time frames; skills, knowledge, and other developmental needs of the new position; and any other issues that might affect the long-term plan.

Development Activities:

- **Formal learning.** State skills and knowledge that the worker needs to develop, courses that might address those needs, and where the worker can find those courses.
- **Informal learning.** Name sources of ongoing education and development for the worker, including periodicals and websites the worker should regularly read, and professional associations and networks that the worker might join.
- **Credentials.** State credentials, such as licenses, certifications, and similar third-party credentials, that the worker needs to achieve the next phase in his or her career and what actions are needed to acquire those credentials.
- **Developmental assignments and activities,** such as informational interviews, internships, volunteer assignments that might prepare the worker for a future job, developmental assignments, and similar activities that can help the worker achieve the career goal stated in the plan.
- **Limiting factors.** List factors that could affect the worker's ability to achieve the career goals identified, such as availability of time and funds for certain activities, and the worker's responsibilities (in terms of both time and money) for achieving the goals identified in the plan.

Regardless of who initiates the process, the extent of structure in preparing for the future varies depending on the work situation and the worker's clarity of mind and enthusiasm for a career change. Although employers can provide workers with coaching, support, information, and other resources at this phase of their work, learning at this touchpoint closely resembles *true* informal learning for most workers.

Touchpoint 8: Preparing Workers for Their Next Jobs

The next touchpoint builds on the previous one—preparing for the next job. Consider the case of Marley, the unfocused junior account executive with an advertising agency who, through mentoring, decided to focus on business-to-business sales. Because she planned a lateral move within the same job category and did not require formal training to make this move, Marley would focus most of her learning on informal efforts, such as reading trade publications and websites about business-to-business sales, speaking to other people who serve the business-to-business market, and when feasible, applying the new knowledge by actively pursuing business-to-business accounts.

The extent of structure applied to the learning at this phase varies based on a combination of factors, such as the nature of the job that workers are preparing for and the extent to which they prefer structured learning. For workers who prepared a formal development plan, that plan often provides the level of structure needed. For workers who did not prepare a formal development plan, establishing some sort of plan at the beginning of this phase might structure activities and keep skill building efforts focused on the intended goal.

For example, the acquisition of formal credentials like degrees, certifications, and training might occur through formal learning. But much of the preparation—even for those pursuing formal degrees—involves informal activities, such as self-development, networking, and mentoring. Some workers might even try using their new skills in their current jobs or through developmental and volunteer assignments. When they feel ready for it, workers also need to begin the process of preparing their resumes and applying for new jobs. Even if they have access to mentors, many workers benefit from formal coaching throughout this preparation process.

Furthermore, workers ultimately need to take the initiative for some of the learning that occurs during this touchpoint. After all, it's their careers.

Touchpoint 9: Addressing Ongoing Organizational Initiatives

In addition to these touchpoints for learning during the life cycle of a job, other learning opportunities may arise as a result of ongoing organizational initiatives. These initiatives include change management programs, quality improvement programs, and mergers. They happen on a schedule determined by senior management and often overlap with learning efforts specific to a phase in the life cycle of the job.

Senior management, working with training and development professionals, usually establish formal learning objectives for these initiatives as well as outcomes they hope to achieve, ideally linking these objectives to broader organizational goals. Not surprisingly, most of the learning associated with ongoing organizational initiatives is formal.

As most change management experts would note, however, the success of these efforts relies not only on achieving the formal learning objectives of the program but in the ability of workers to integrate the goals into their own work. Although formal learning initiates this integration, actual integration only happens through informal learning efforts.

This integration typically involves two efforts, which establish the goals for informal learning at this phase. In the first, workers determine how the initiative affects them. This assessment usually happens informally, often without structure. For example, workers might notice that processes work more smoothly or that a problem arises that the change team did not anticipate.

The second way in which workers integrate the change initiative is by determining how they feel about it. For example, if the formal learning program suggests that the initiative should simplify processes, workers' impressions about the organizational initiative will be shaped by the extent to which they see simpler processes.

Training and development professionals might feel inclined to formalize and structure the transfer of learning about the ongoing organizational initiative. To some extent, they can. In addition to preparing a formal training program associated with the initiative, professionals can prepare resources to help workers transfer the initiative to the context of their jobs. Acting as performance consultants—like those described in Harold Stolovitch and Erica Keeps's *Training Ain't Performance* (2004)—training and development professionals can also identify and remove obstacles to implementation.

In the end, however, workers complete the integration either on their own or in collaboration with their co-workers. That, in turn, shapes not only how the initiative is integrated but how workers feel about it. These on-the-job experiences usually include interactions with documentation like user's guides, policies, and procedures developed for the initiative, hands-on practice, and conversations with others who influence workers' perceptions of the change.

Applying This Framework

Informal learning plays a significant role in the ongoing learning, development, and performance improvement of workers as they become more familiar and experienced in their jobs, because as workers develop that familiarity and experience, they can better identify their own developmental needs and have the motivation to manage them—sometimes entirely on their own, sometimes with support from managers and colleagues.

Training and development professionals can use the framework presented in this chapter to determine the types of needs workers have at a given touchpoint, and determine the extents to which formal and informal learning might address those needs and strengthen performance.

Getting It Done

Worksheet 3–1 guides you through applying this framework in the context of your organization. It first prompts you to choose the touchpoint, then suggests questions to consider as you choose formal and informal learning activities to address needs related to that touchpoint.

Worksheet 3–1. Questions to Consider When Choosing Learning Experiences Associated With a Touchpoint

1. Where in the life cycles of their jobs are most of the workers facing this particular challenge of learning, development, or performance improvement? (Circle one)
   a. Orient workers to the technical aspects of a job.
   b. Onboard workers to the culture and values of the group.
   c. Expand the scope of assignments a worker can handle.
   d. Build workers' proficiency.
   e. Help workers address undocumented challenges.
   f. Update workers' skills and knowledge.
   g. Help workers choose career goals.
   h. Prepare workers for their next jobs.
   i. Address ongoing organizational initiatives.

2. Which specific learning, development, and performance improvement needs do workers have? This question, in turn, might initiate several related questions, such as these:

   a. Can the content be explicitly taught? The material addressed at some touchpoints in the learning process is less explicit than others and, therefore, most likely learned informally. *Tip:* For example, material about corporate culture and handling undocumented problems is less explicit than introductory technical content for a job.

   _____
   _____
   _____
   _____

b. What is the time to performance needed? The more quickly employers need workers to reach a given performance level, the more likely the need for formal learning.

_____

_____

_____

_____

c. Which workers need to develop skills? *Tip:* Studies such as those of the University of Toronto's Institute for Work and Lifelong Learning suggest that the higher a worker's educational and occupational level, the more likely he or she is to learn informally (Livingstone, 2010).

_____

_____

_____

_____

d. How much can employers rely on workers to learn on their own? *Tip:* Motivation of learners plays a significant role in this. The more motivated the learner is to explore the subject, the more likely it is that he or she will learn the content informally.

_____

_____

_____

_____

e. Assuming that informal learning can play a role in addressing the learning, development, or performance improvement need, which specific combinations of formal and informal learning and development activities can support workers in addressing this challenge?

_____

_____

_____

_____

f. What support do workers need to successfully master this particular learning, development, or performance improvement challenge?

_____

_____

_____

_____

Worksheet 3–2 presents common scenarios in which workers at different touchpoints in their jobs must address learning and development needs. Given what you have learned in this chapter, try to identify the touchpoints the workers have reached in each scenario, and then devise informal learning solutions to address their needs.

Worksheet 3–2. Applying the Framework

How can you appropriately integrate informal learning at different phases of the life span of a job? Try this exercise to find out.

1. Your manager has asked you to develop a "creative program" for slightly experienced customer service representatives in the call center of an online retailer. The workers will have successfully completed the probation period (60 days) by mastering the most basic calls—orders in the books and music department. Your manager says that the workers will be ready to handle more complicated calls, including orders for clothing, shoes, or electronics. Your manager suggested that you develop an advanced three-day class for all of these representatives but has said, "I'm open to other ideas." Given what you have learned about learning and the life cycle of a job, can you think of other ideas?

   _____

   _____

   _____

   _____

   _____

Debriefing of exercise 1: This experience occurs at the third touchpoint in the cycle: Expand the scope of assignments a worker can handle. Because workers are learning new skills that must be applied in a particular way—that is, learning goals and measures of success are externally defined—much structure is needed. But because different workers will be assigned to different types of calls—some to clothing, some to shoes, and some to electronics—a single, formal training program seems inappropriate. Most workers will snooze through the two-thirds of the program that does not relate to them.

Workers need to learn about the product lines they will be supporting, as well as how to answer particular sales and support questions that customers might pose to them (and that can probably be anticipated), so formal instructional materials might be helpful. These materials extend existing skills and knowledge, so they can be made for self-study.

Workers also need to be able to recall knowledge when answering more complex phone inquiries, so on-the-job mentoring might also be helpful.

Because a high level of structure is needed for workers to master goals that are externally defined and for which success is also externally defined, *true* informal learning is not appropriate. But because the content lends itself to self-study and mentoring, some type of informal learning could be efficient and effective.

2. Within the next month, the latest version of the software for creating e-learning courses will be installed on all of the computers in the training and development department. The new software is essentially the same as the old software, but it offers several new options for editing the recordings of the programs. For example, after recording the narration to a PowerPoint slide show, e-learning developers can now add music, insert wipes, fades, and other transitional effects between scenes, and add credits at the end of the program—much like a movie. The manager of the IT group suggests that you prepare a one-day training program to introduce these changes but has said, "I'm open to other ideas." Given what you have learned about learning and the life cycle of a job, can you think of other ideas?

_____

_____

_____

_____

_____

Debriefing of exercise 2: This experience occurs at the sixth touchpoint in the cycle: Update workers' skills and knowledge. In this case, workers need to adjust to a new release of authoring software. From the description of the situation, the primary changes involve providing workers with additional capabilities. Workers will continue to perform tasks they already perform without any changes. That means that, even if the workers do not learn anything about the new version of the software, they can continue to perform their work. This also suggests that extensive formal training is probably overkill.

Rather, workers should learn about the new capabilities as they need them. What workers need at first is awareness of those new capabilities and occasional reminders of them, in case they overlook the first announcement or forget about it. As workers recognize a need to use a new capability, the need for learning arises. On-demand materials that can guide workers through the performance of the new tasks can probably meet the need. Establishing a help line might also be useful for those workers who prefer someone to guide them through using the new capabilities for the first time.

4

How Can Training and Development Professionals Support Informal Learning?

- -

 What's Inside This Chapter

In this chapter, you'll learn

▶ about the central role that support plays in informal learning
▶ how to support informal learning at the organizational and individual levels.

As explored in previous chapters, informal learning offers many benefits, including the ability to offer learning opportunities that suit workers' schedules and are tailored to the unique circumstances and interests of workers. But informal learning also presents a number of challenges, including workers learning material incorrectly when studying on their own, choosing to finish studying before they have actually mastered the content, lacking the motivation to continue learning, and receiving no acknowledgment for their studies.

59

So what can training and development professionals do to maximize the benefits and minimize the liabilities of informal learning? More specifically, how can training and development professionals help organizations integrate, acknowledge, and support the informal learning that occurs to better realize the full benefits of it? This chapter addresses these questions by first exploring the central role that support plays in informal learning and then exploring practical ways training and development professionals can establish a framework of support for workers in their informal learning efforts.

The Role of Support in Informal Learning

As a training and development professional, your role in the informal learning process often differs substantially from the more familiar roles you play as an instructor or instructional designer. Rather, in informal learning, training and development professionals play the roles of of facilitator and supporter—adapting existing materials designed and produced by others rather than designing, developing, and presenting new materials. Four key concepts illustrate these roles.

Concept 1: Play the Role of Grandparent

Many formally trained learning professionals take a directive, almost paternalistic approach to training. Like parents who want the best for their children, these training and development professionals are convinced that if they set formal learning objectives, sequence instructional material for maximum learning, and use tests as assessments of learning, then workers will successfully master the content.

If formal learning has a certain parental quality, informal learning has grandparenting qualities—that is, it involves refraining from giving advice unless specifically asked to do so. Training and development professionals show a similar restraint with informal learning because it usually occurs at the initiative of the worker, and that worker may or may not consult training and development professionals for advice. In these situations, training and development professionals can only make all parties aware that they are available to support informal learning efforts. Workers might then seek advice, such as tips on the availability of resources such as websites and experts that support informal learning.

Sometimes training and development professionals do need to play a more direct role in informal learning, such as using design and instructional skills to prepare materials intended to support informal learning efforts. In such instances, training and development professionals recognize that despite their intentions, workers and managers might use the materials in different ways than were originally intended in the design if the learning goals differ from those guiding the design of the program.

Concept 2: Play the Role of Coach

Sometimes informal learning means that training and development professionals need to become coaches and help workers and managers past their trouble spots to achieve their goals for informal learning. In such cases, training and development professionals bring three unique talents:

- ▶ skills in clarifying goals and desired outcomes, which help managers and workers focus on challenges
- ▶ planning and organizational skills, which help managers and workers identify gaps in their knowledge and skills and devise paths toward bridging those gaps
- ▶ knowledge of available resources, which directs managers and workers to specific informal learning and development opportunities.

Concept 3: Avoid the Role of Designer

If formal training courses were fashion, they would be *haute couture*—the high fashion that is custom designed by artisans for use by the few people who can afford it. As top fashion designers control all aspects of the design and creation of their runway masterpieces, so training and development professionals control all aspects of the design and creation of training programs. In contrast, informal learning is like *prêt-à-porter*—ready-to-wear or off-the-rack fashion. Rather than being custom designed for each situation, materials used for informal learning are mass produced, and workers mix and match them to suit their individual needs. And as people need to take in a waistline and a hem to make sure the clothing fits perfectly, so workers need to adjust content with information from their own environments so that it accurately addresses their work conditions.

Think About This

Like *haute couture*, formal training has a comparatively high price tag. One of the reasons that informal learning costs so much less than formal learning is that informal learning leverages existing materials and relationships. For example, a worker might check a reference manual or consult a knowledgeable co-worker to learn how to solve an immediate work problem. Because the reference already exists and the knowledgeable co-worker is already available, no additional expense is incurred.

Although some resources for informal learning are designed and developed by training and development professionals, the majority are not. In fact, these resources are often prepared by technical writers, engineers, human resources specialists, product managers, and others with technical knowledge.

Similarly, as off-the-rack fashion is often worn in ways not initially intended by the designer, workers often use informal learning resources differently than the creators intended. For example, a software user might cut out a chart from a user's guide, paste it on her wall, and use it as an ongoing reminder about important information she uses every day.

Concept 4: Informal Learning Within the Context of the ASTD Competency Model

Informal learning plays an important role in the ASTD Competency Model (ASTD, 2010), which defines the knowledge and skills needed by professionals in this field and underlies the Certified Professional in Learning and Performance (CPLP) designation. Two *Areas of Expertise* competencies address informal learning.

The first of these two competencies that address informal learning is managing organizational knowledge. Managing organizational knowledge involves working with stakeholders in an organization to identify critical content, making sure that content is documented and readily available to all who need it (and protected from those who should not have access to it), and making sure that the content is current, so people are working with up-to-date information. Figure 4–1 shows the managing organizational knowledge competency within the broader framework of the ASTD Competency Model.

The second of the competencies used in supporting informal learning is coaching, which involves identifying the challenges that individuals face as they try to

Figure 4–1. Informal Learning Competencies Within the ASTD Competency Model

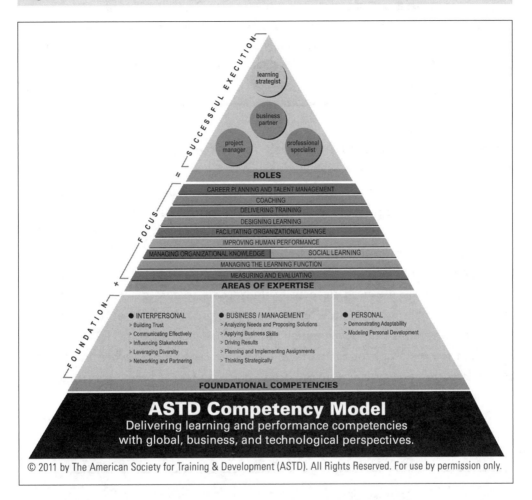

© 2011 by The American Society for Training & Development (ASTD). All Rights Reserved. For use by permission only.

achieve an informal learning goal and provides the support, guidance, and feedback needed to achieve that goal. Figure 4–1 also shows the coaching competency within the broader framework of the ASTD Competency Model.

The next two sections of this chapter explore specific issues that will likely arise as you try to adapt to the two key roles of training and development professionals in supporting informal learning—(role a) providing a framework for informal learning in the organization and (role b) supporting individual workers in their informal learning efforts.

Basic Rule

The basic competencies required by training and development professionals who work with informal learning are managing organizational knowledge and coaching, rather than designing learning and delivering training.

Role A: Providing a Framework for Informal Learning in the Organization

In the first of their two roles in supporting informal learning, training and development professionals provide the framework for informal learning in their organizations. They need to negotiate for a role in guiding informal learning efforts in their organizations, as several other groups also want to play this role, such as communications, human resources, and information technology groups. Training and development professionals also need to identify the specific resources needed for informal learning and, if necessary, request funds to support the acquisition of these resources. In addition, training and development professionals help identify the content and consider the easiest way for the workers to gain access to it and, when needed, prepare related resources such as templates that let content experts easily share their knowledge in a clear, accessible way.

What follows are eight specific measures that training and development professionals can take to fill this role.

Basic Rule

Before informal learning can flourish at the individual level, resources and support must exist at the organizational level.

1. Set Clear Expectations About Informal Learning

The first way to support informal learning in a workplace is to set clear expectations among stakeholders about what informal learning is and its capacity for affecting workers. Training and development professionals might believe that this requires hard numbers. But such hard numbers do not exist because the research has not yet produced indisputable evidence about gains in learning. This lack of hard numbers might not pose as serious a problem as some might think. Some research suggests that senior management recognizes that hard numbers are not always feasible with a "soft" discipline like training and development (Carliner, Qayyum, Sanchez-Lozano, and Macmillan, 2007; O'Driscoll, Sugrue, and Vona, 2005).

The research suggests, too, that executives positively respond to demonstrated benefits of informal learning, including these:

- ▶ It supplements formal training through application to the job.
- ▶ It develops expertise by letting workers tailor knowledge, skills, and attitudes learned to the unique circumstances of their jobs.
- ▶ It offers flexibility, so workers learn when the need arises and at their convenience.
- ▶ It supports career development efforts by providing workers with the opportunity to explore their own interests on their own time.
- ▶ It supports the sharing of tacit knowledge.
- ▶ It helps workers integrate into their role in an organization.
- ▶ It can reduce some training costs by leveraging existing relationships and content intended for other uses rather than designing and developing new programs.

Despite these solidly demonstrated benefits and real claims you can make, avoid suggesting unsubstantiated or misleading benefits of informal learning, such as:

- ▶ "Informal learning replaces formal learning." In many instances, formal learning remains the most appropriate approach, especially when workers must perform tasks in a particular way or develop a skill on a predetermined schedule. A more realistic claim is that informal learning complements and extends formal learning.
- ▶ "Informal learning is more effective than classroom learning." No evidence exists either to support or refute this claim.
- ▶ "Informal learning is natural, so it therefore is more appropriate than formal learning." Informal learning *is* natural, but learners tend to explore topics of interest to them and learn what they choose to learn, which may or may not

match the needs of the organization; in addition, the material may not be learned accurately.

▶ "Informal learning will result in significant cost savings for the organization." In some cases it can. But you should estimate both the costs and savings on a case-by-case basis. You may find that savings are modest; or, if savings over formal learning do exist, an associated risk might also exist that, in turn, creates a potential cost.

2. Gain Executive Support for Informal Learning Efforts

One consistent conclusion of research on informal learning in the workplace is that a key factor in its success is the tangible support of executives in the organization. Executive support takes many forms; each one contributes differently to informal learning.

The first is a formal statement in support of informal learning activities. Such a statement acknowledges that workers learn many aspects of their jobs informally and indicates that executives support such processes. The statement should also promote awareness of informal learning and encourage workers to participate in it.

The next form of support involves approval of funding for proposed projects related to informal learning and, before approving funding, providing supportive feedback on draft proposals. For example, suppose that a team requests funding for a social networking application that could promote exchanges among workers throughout the organization and, in the process, learning. Ideally, executives would fund that proposal. If executives feel they cannot do so, they could provide specific feedback about their concerns, so that a future draft would address those concerns and prove itself fundable.

A third form of executive support for informal learning involves approving the use of work time for informal learning activities. For example, instead of chiding workers for wasting their time around the watercooler, executives might formally acknowledge that important information gets exchanged in these impromptu conversations and encourage more social interactions.

Most significantly, executives can support informal learning by participating in it themselves and talking about it in their interactions with workers. Such participation models the desired behavior, which is one of the most powerful messages of support that executives can send to workers.

3. Help Build an Internal Infrastructure of Content That Workers Can Leverage for Informal Learning

Much of the content needed for work-related informal learning specifically pertains to the organization. Workers typically turn to these types of organizational documents to learn informally:

- ▸ policies, procedures, and processes, which individual departments, functions (groups of departments), divisions, and entire organizations typically prepare
- ▸ guidelines and standards
- ▸ marketing literature, user documents, and service documents about current products
- ▸ planning documents about future products
- ▸ customer and service records.

But one of the most persistent problems in organizations is that no one has documented information, or if they have, it is inaccessible to workers who need it. The documents might be stored on the hard drive of an individual's computer instead of in a shared folder that all workers can access. Or workers might have access to the documents but be unable to read them because the workers who created them use codes and similar shorthand notations that only the author and perhaps a co-worker or two might comprehend. Even when it does exist, much of the content is out of date.

Organizations that have little, if any, current documentation often feel overwhelmed by the sheer volume of the task of creating it. Even when the motivation to document this material exists, workers often lack the time to do so. Workers in customer service departments, for example, are assessed by the amount of time they spend in direct interaction with customers. Although documenting policies, procedures, processes, and similar material is work-related, it is a secondary administrative task and takes time from the primary responsibility on which workers are assessed.

When workers do have the motivation and the time, they often lack the skill. For example, the primary competency of customer service representatives is interacting with clients to take their orders, answer their questions, and solve their problems—not writing policies and procedures. Indeed, many do not even like to write.

Training and development professionals can promote practical measures like these to address each of these issues:

▶ Establish shared spaces for all workers to provide and access content. Organizations often use shared folders on a server to make information available to everyone. More recently, organizations have turned to *cloud computing*, in which the shared folder or disk is available through the web rather than an internal network, and is thus more readily available to people. Organizations have also turned to content management systems, which maintain project archives, oversee the approval process for content to be published on the web, and secure information from unauthorized access.

▶ Make sharing content a job responsibility, and periodically audit information to make sure that workers are fulfilling this responsibility.

▶ Tackle the project of documentation in parts. Consider documenting the policies, procedures, processes, and guidelines followed on just one project or product line at a time.

▶ Have training and development professionals, or others with skills in documenting processes, write the content for the department or function in need; or develop templates that guide workers through the process of documenting their content, so they can do so on their own. Figure 4–2 provides an example of a template for a process description.

Figure 4–2. Example of a Template for a Process Description

Part	How to Write It
Introduce the procedure.	1. First, state the goal of the procedure as succinctly as possible. 2. If readers need knowledge, supplies, or assistance to perform the procedure, next state that information in a "Read Me First" section, which precedes the procedure. 3. Present supplies needed as a check-off list. The checkbox signals readers that they need to do something. 4. Only explain "must-know" terminology and concepts in a procedure. Readers use procedures to learn how to do something, not to learn the concepts and terminology underlying them. 5. Mention "Who should perform the procedure." 6. Provide an estimate of the time needed to complete the procedure.

Present the steps of the procedure.	Consider these guidelines as you write a procedure:
	
	• Write procedures as numbered lists. That is, begin each step with a number. The number tells readers the sequence for performing the steps.
	
	• Because users can handle only a limited amount of information at any given time, limit the length to 10 steps. If your procedure has more steps, break them into a "mini-procedure" within the larger procedure.
	
	• Consider the following when writing the steps in a procedure:
	
	  • Limit each step in a procedure to one task.
	
	  • Present conditional information as a clause at the beginning of a step; do not place it after the action. For example, if users need to use both hands to hold a piece in place on an assembly line, say it at the beginning of the step, like this:
	
	    Holding the piece with both hands, place the assembly in the drying machine.
	
	  Do not write the clause like this:
	
	    Place the assembly in the drying machine and hold it with both hands.
	
	  • For tasks that users are expected to perform, write in the imperative mood. That is, begin with an action verb and tell readers what to do.
	
	  • For procedures that users are not expected to perform, include the agent (the person who is expected to perform the task) for each action so readers know who or what is responsible for that task. For example:
	
	    The Information Development department will distribute the information plan by January 22.
	
	  Rather than:
	
	    The information plan will be distributed by January 22.
	
	  • When several people perform a procedure together, you need to state who performs each step and how responsibility passes among people performing the procedure. For example:
	
	  1. The technical writer writes the document.
	  2. The technical writer electronically transmits the document to the editor.
	  3. The technical editor:
	    a. Prints the document.
	    b. Identifies the passages that need to be illustrated.
	    c. Completes an Art Request Form for each illustration needed.
	    d. Submits the Art Request Forms to the technical illustrator.

Close the procedure.	1. Tell users that the procedure is complete.
	2. Name anticipated problems and suggest how to address them.
	Note that you should describe anticipated problems at the place they would likely occur, so users receive immediate feedback and can easily correct problems themselves.
	3. Refer users to related procedures and other information of interest.

4. Secure External Content to Extend the Opportunities for Informal Learning

In addition to internal content, workers often need access to material from outside sources, such as

- ▶ industry research conducted by consultants and trade groups
- ▶ trade and professional magazines and journals
- ▶ databases that provide access to trade and professional magazines and journals
- ▶ webinars and online events sponsored by trade and professional associations and private organizations
- ▶ online tutorials provided by trade associations, professional associations, and private providers
- ▶ books and series of books, in both text and audiobook format.

This externally published material places information in the broader context of the industry and economy and provides independent research data on competitors, product areas, and the industry. Training and development professionals can ensure that workers have access to these essential resources by including the funding for the subscriptions, tuition, and purchases of this material in their budgets.

After acquiring the externally published content, training and development professionals can help ensure that workers have access to it by working with the groups that establish policies on use of the Internet in the workplace. The goal should be to promote sensible policies that provide workers with unimpeded access to external resources when using them supports their work.

5. *Continually Promote the Availability of Resources for Informal Learning*

Workers cannot take advantage of informal learning opportunities if they do not know they exist, especially those opportunities that involve a conscious learning effort. So organizations need to constantly remind workers that informal learning resources and opportunities exist. A complete marketing program includes the following components:

- ▶ Collateral, which are catalogs that identify the key categories of resources, list and describe each learning resource available, and describe the intended or possible uses and audiences for each resource. Typically, organizations publish this material online through a learning portal or similar website. But some organizations also produce print materials, such as brochures for distribution in meetings with groups. Printed materials typically describe informal learning opportunities in a broad way and direct readers to a website for specific resources and opportunities.

- ▶ Promotional materials, which provide short-term visibility for one or more informal learning resources. Typical examples of promotional materials include these:
  - ▶ announcement of a new resource, such as a subscription to a database like EBSCO or the availability of an updated product catalog
  - ▶ promotion of an individual set of resources to raise awareness of them, such as promotion of a series of tutorials on project management or a subscription to the electronic resources of the Harvard Business School Press
  - ▶ general awareness of learning in the workplace, such as organizational events scheduled in conjunction with Learn@Work week sponsored by the Canadian Society for Training and Development
  - ▶ a newsletter or webzine, a regularly published promotional vehicle that condenses several announcements into a single publication.

In addition to promoting specific resources, training and development groups might also include materials about how to make more effective use of informal learning.

Many organizations distribute these promotional materials online, through email (for formal communications), social media (for quick, informal communications), and websites (which people learn about through email and social media messages that direct people to them).

You might also use other media, such as posters, table cards placed on tables in employee cafeterias and similar public gathering spaces, videos, and even fortune cookies with custom-published fortunes that lead people to informal learning resources.

Because informal learning fits into a workday that is crowded not only with activity but also with other important information and messages, a single promotional message often fails to gain attention. Training and development professionals should regularly promote informal learning opportunities to increase the likelihood that workers think of informal learning when the need for it arises.

Basic Rule

Although informal learning leverages existing resources and relationships, it does require particular investments. For example, without content (because it does not exist, the organization lacks a subscription, or the IT group blocked it), workers have limited learning opportunities. Without awareness of the resources, workers might not take advantage of them. So plan to invest in documentation, subscriptions and tuition, and promotion.

6. Emphasize Ongoing Learning Through Performance Planning and Evaluation, Regular Skills Assessments, and Career Planning

The performance planning and evaluation process provides a specific opportunity to emphasize the link between ongoing learning efforts—informal and formal—and successful performance on the job. Specifically, these milestones in the performance planning and evaluation process provide opportunities to promote informal learning:

▶ The job description, which forms the basis of recruiting efforts. The description might tell prospective workers that one of the responsibilities of the job involves ongoing learning and can even suggest the nature of the learning involved, such as keeping up-to-date on product launches or tracking developments in the industry.

▶ The job interview, which provides managers an opportunity to find out about candidates' informal learning attitudes and processes.

▶ The performance plan, which states not only specific expectations of job performance but also specific expectations for learning. Some organizations focus on the quantity of training. Many high-technology companies focus on a particular number of hours, while healthcare organizations often focus on accumulating a given number of continuing education units (CEUs). Such efforts tend to focus on formal training. But recently developed certification maintenance programs for the CPLP, as well as the certifications offered by the International Society for Performance Improvement and the Canadian Society for Training and Development, encourage informal learning by offering credit for it. Employers might incorporate these ideas into their own learning plans.

▶ Informal performance reviews, which provide an opportunity to discuss what workers have learned and how they did so—as well as what they need to learn.

▶ Formal performance reviews, which provide an opportunity to take an inventory of all learning activities—not just formal classes, but less formal activities like lectures, conferences, and lunch and learns—and individual efforts, such as ongoing reading, and unconscious activities. See the next section of this chapter for suggestions of specific techniques for eliciting learning from informal and unconscious activities.

▶ Career development plans, which provide an opportunity to clarify medium- and long-term plans and identify the range of experiences for achieving those goals. Achieving medium- and long-term career goals often involves informal learning.

Although each of these milestones provides an opportunity to discuss informal learning, they do not necessarily shift responsibility for informal learning from the worker to the employer. Rather, these conversations merely provide an opportunity to formally raise the issue of informal learning. As workers become more experienced in their jobs, managers should increasingly look to these workers to identify and fulfill their own learning needs.

7. *Maintain Content*

One of the key tasks in providing support for informal learning involves regularly updating the internal content used for it. That task is not always easy. Here are some typical reasons for that difficulty:

▷ Much of the content that workers use for informal learning is developed by groups other than training and development. For example, product development and marketing groups typically "own" information about products, while human resources typically "owns" company policies and procedures.

▷ Members of the organization often have a difficult time finding all of the information that needs to be updated. For example, several versions of a description on how to perform a particular manufacturing task might exist—one in the engineers' process description, one in the process manual for workers on the line, and another in an ISO 9000 application. Most organizations do not maintain an inventory of all of their content, and as a result, one source might be updated while the other two are overlooked.

▷ Documenting current projects often receives priority over maintaining older content, especially content intended for internal use. For example, if you need to develop a course about a brand new product, updating information about a current product often becomes a lower priority assignment.

Organizations can take several measures to address these difficulties. One is instituting the use of content management systems. Content management systems let organizations store and organize content in files, distinguish among different versions of the same file, and track the process of developing content—from inception through approvals to publication. These systems can address many of the issues described above by providing a single source file for content—that is, they maintain a single file with information about a particular piece of content and use that single file to produce all of the related content on that subject.

Most significantly, however, when organizations give workers responsibility for preparing content, they must also provide these workers with time to maintain it and assess workers on the extent to which they have kept content current.

8. Advocate for the Resources Needed to Learn Informally on the Job

Training and development professionals should advocate for investments in the systems and processes needed to make learning resources available.

One of the processes for which training and development professionals should advocate is an organization-wide *information architecture*, a means of structuring content so people can store it in a consistent way and workers can easily locate and read it. An effective information architecture involves standards for labeling, organizing, and structuring content online. For example, training and development professionals might advocate for a convention for labeling content, a process called *meta-tagging*, that facilitates searching by providing users with a known set of search terms.

Another process for which training and development professionals should advocate is letting workers participate in learning activities during work hours. Managers are often reluctant to let workers do so because they fear that if workers are not working on immediate projects, they are not being productive. They must also consider that hourly workers who study work-related topics on their own time are probably eligible for overtime payments. Research also suggests that workers themselves feel guilty using work time to learn.

Training and development professionals should also advocate for work time to use social media. While tweeting or using Facebook during work hours might seem like a time-waster to managers, those tweets and status updates are often work-related and could ultimately benefit the organization.

In most instances, training and development professionals play an advisory role in the matters just discussed as they have little, if any, ability to make these resources available themselves. They rely instead on influencing others in the organization to provide these resources. That's the reason that the term *advocate* rather than *acquire* is used in the name of this measure.

Think About This

When considering the infrastructure for informal learning, approach informal learning systemically rather than as an isolated event or project. As noted earlier, informal learning is about a process of development that occurs over a period of time and through which workers gradually adjust their job performance by leveraging materials and experiences already available on the job.

Role B: Supporting Individual Workers in Their Informal Learning Efforts

In the second of their two roles in supporting informal learning, training and development professionals support individual workers with their informal learning efforts. Specifically in this role, training and development professionals help workers and their managers clarify goals around informal learning, identify their strengths and weaknesses so that the workers themselves can meaningfully address them, inspire workers through the sometimes lonely process of participating in informal learning, and help workers and their managers acquire institutional and external support, when needed, for informal learning. Following are 10 ways that training and development professionals can support informal learning.

Basic Rule

Although materials and resources used in informal learning are provided throughout the organization, each learning experience is tailored to the needs of the individual—from choosing the goals and path through learning, to continuing with the level of support provided during the learning process, to closing with the means of assessing and recognizing informal learning efforts.

1. When Feasible, Let Workers Lead Their Own Learning Efforts

One of the benefits of informal learning is its potential to deliver powerful learning experiences, in which people experience changes on both intellectual and emotional levels. Such learning often emerges from achieving goals that learners set for themselves.

Observing workers as they attempt to establish their own goals and plans for achieving them is often frustrating for formally trained professionals in our field, whose natural inclination is to develop clearly stated, measurable goals for workers and suggest clear paths toward achieving those goals. But workers need to go through this process on their own, even when the need to learn comes from external sources, because identifying their own needs and setting their own goals is as much a part of the learning experience as learning the material itself.

2. Help Workers Clarify Their Learning Goals and the Paths Toward Those Goals

Researcher Michael Eraut (2000) found that 80 percent of workers had a general idea of what they wanted to achieve through their informal learning efforts. These workers typically took an "emergent strategy" toward their informal learning, taking advantage of learning opportunities as they presented themselves. Training and development professionals can strengthen this emergent strategy preferred by many workers by helping them clarify their goals and linking the goals to learning opportunities.

Training and development professionals can help workers establish goals by:

▶ Clarifying their needs. Sometimes workers start their informal learning efforts with vague goals, which works well in some instances. However, when workers expect significant rewards for their learning efforts, such as promotions and raises, they benefit from identifying exactly what they plan to achieve and how it benefits the employer.

▶ Exploring the implications of achieving their goals. In some instances, workers have not fully thought through the implications of their own goals. As a result, they might learn that achieving one goal would cause an unexpected disruption in another aspect of their lives or careers. For example, an introverted worker might have a career goal of becoming a manager without realizing that management is essentially a "people" job.

▶ Exploring the motivation behind their goals. For example, expectations of others often drive career decisions, such as parents or spouses encouraging workers to take promotions for greater pay. In some instances, the workers have no interest in achieving such goals.

Training and development professionals can also help workers link learning opportunities with their goals. For example, to help workers determine what to learn, offer annotated lists of resources. These lists direct workers to articles, books, blogs, websites, and similar resources on a topic of interest.

A **basic list** merely lists resources about a topic. Online resources contain links; offline resources contain complete bibliographic information. This type of list helps workers who already have a level of familiarity with a field or want to assess resources for themselves. The example in Figure 4–3 shows a sample of a basic list of resources.

Figure 4–3. Basic List of Resources

Technical Writing

- Markel, M. (2007). *Technical Communication* (8th ed.). Boston: Bedford/St. Martin's.
- The Technical Communicators Resource Site, http://www.techcommunicators.com/techcomm/index.html
- Writing Guidelines, http://www.writing.engr.psu.edu/
- The Online Writing Lab (OWL) at Purdue, http://owl.english.purdue.edu/owl/

An **annotated list of resources** provides comments on each of the resources, indicating the type of material that each addresses. This type of list helps workers who have limited familiarity with a topic and need advice on the value of different resources. Figure 4–4 shows an annotated list of resources.

Figure 4–4. Annotated List of Resources

Technical Writing

- Markel, M. (2007). *Technical Communication* (8th ed.). Boston: Bedford/St. Martin's (a textbook that provides insights into the process of writing and instruction on writing common types of technical content)
- The Technical Communicators Resource Site (resources for professional technical communicators compiled by a working technical writer based in British Columbia) http://www.techcommunicators.com/techcomm/index.html
- Writing Guidelines (provides advice for handling specific types of challenges that arise when writing; says that the guidelines are intended for engineering and science students but really apply to all types of educational and technical writing situations) http://www.writing.engr.psu.edu/
- The Online Writing Lab (OWL) at Purdue (provides answers to specific questions about writing technical content) http://owl.english.purdue.edu/owl/

A **list of resources for accomplishing particular objectives** describes the primary goal that a resource helps workers achieve. This type of list benefits a worker who has little familiarity with a topic or is still forming his or her learning goals and would like some guidance about which resource to choose and when. Figure 4–5 shows a list of resources for accomplishing particular objectives.

Figure 4–5. Resources for Accomplishing Particular Objectives

Technical Writing

- To develop basic technical writing skills, check out Markel, M. (2007). *Technical Communication* (8th ed.). Boston: Bedford/St. Martin's.

- To learn about the profession of technical communication, visit http://www.techcommunicators.com/techcomm/index.html

- To learn how to handle certain grammatical situations, citations, and similar mechanical issues, visit Writing Guidelines at http://www.writing.engr.psu.edu/

- To receive answers to questions about grammar and style, visit the Online Writing Lab (OWL) at Purdue: http://owl.english.purdue.edu/owl/

For advice on how to use learning resources, consider preparing road maps, which provide workers with a visual map linking various resources for the purpose of achieving a larger learning outcome. See the road map in Figure 4–6 for an example.

Figure 4–6. Sample of a Curriculum Road Map

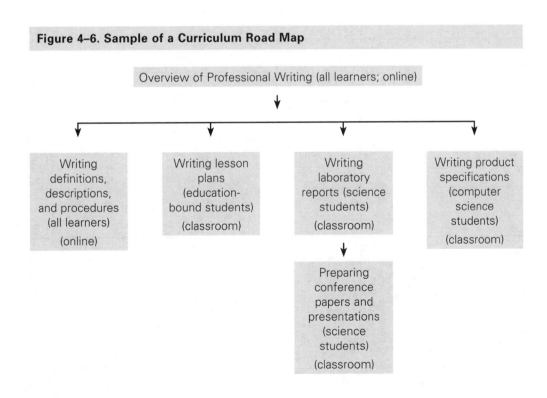

Although road maps help workers see pathways through the content, they are meant for a general audience. Individualized learning plans, by contrast, provide a framework for a particular worker to consider his or her learning goals and the resources and experiences that would best help achieve those goals. Workers can complete these plans on their own or with a manager, senior worker, or similar coach. Figure 4–7 shows a template for an individualized learning plan.

Figure 4–7. Sample of an Individualized Learning Plan

Individualized Learning Plan for:					
What you hope to learn	Why you want to learn it	How you plan to learn the content	How you plan to experience the content	How you plan to reflect on the content	How you plan to demonstrate that you learned it

3. Help Workers Develop Independent Study and Research Skills

Training and development professionals, managers, and senior workers who coach workers in informal learning efforts need to help workers strengthen their independent study skills. Means of doing so include:

 ▶ Conducting readiness assessments, which evaluate the independent study skills of workers as well as their experience and comfort with using computers and other technologies for learning (Leigh and Watkins, 2005). These assessments provide an overall recommendation of workers' readiness, but also identify specific self-study and technology skills that need development so workers are best positioned to benefit from the independent study experience.

 ▶ Conducting workshops on searching for, and assessing, information on the Internet. Workers rely heavily on Google and similar search engines to find content to inform their work. But research suggests that workers do not always search effectively or critically assess the results for accuracy and appropriateness. In the end, such searches often fail to answer the question driving the search, or fail to provide the most meaningful responses.

 ▶ Coaching workers as challenges arise in the learning process, such as difficulty understanding something and un-learning old content. A measure discussed later in this chapter addresses coaching in more detail.

 ▶ Providing signposts for workers so they can chart their learning progress and unambiguously assess the extent to which they have learned the content. Another measure discussed later in this chapter addresses signposts in more detail.

4. Help Workers Develop Collaborative Working Skills

Although much informal learning occurs independently, much of it also occurs in collaboration with others. The next chapter explores specific ways that workers learn (sometimes unintentionally) through interactions with others.

Because the competencies for working collaboratively are rooted in abstract concepts and involve attitudes as much as behaviors, training and development professionals often label these skills as "soft skills." But the signs of such competencies are often quite visible and concrete in workers in the following situations:

- ▶ brainstorming ideas in a group without judgment of ideas
- ▶ listening to—and absorbing—the explanations of others, which often results in changing workers' views of situations
- ▶ letting go of a preferred approach to work when others demonstrate that another approach is more effective
- ▶ returning the favor of learning from others by sharing knowledge and expertise.

The ASTD Competency Model identifies five interpersonal competencies for collaborating with others: building trust, communicating effectively, influencing stakeholders, leveraging diversity, and networking and partnering. All of these skills are valuable for supporting good teamwork. Here are some ways in which training and development professionals can provide managers with tools to support teams:

- ▶ encourage managers to provide teams with clear mandates
- ▶ provide resources that support team processes, such as templates to document mandates for teams, record agendas for meetings, prepare status reports, and document team guidelines and processes
- ▶ provide an ear and advice when challenges arise in the normal course of teamwork.

5. Help Workers Set Realistic Expectations for Informal Learning Efforts

As noted earlier, one of the ways in which training and development professionals support informal learning involves helping workers consider the implications of their goals. In the process of doing so, training and development professionals also help workers consider whether those goals are realistic. Here are some ways to help workers establish realistic expectations of informal learning:

- ▶ Establish realistic expectations of the time needed to learn. Even rough estimates can help workers plan appropriately. For example, if a particular activity is likely to take four hours, workers realize they need to plan further ahead than they might need to do to accommodate a 15- to 30-minute activity.

▶ Establish clear expectations of workers' responsibilities in the informal learning experience. Some workers might enter learning experiences with the expectation that these experiences are self-contained. For example:

  ▶ Workers might start academic courses without realizing that they require outside reading and homework.

  ▶ Workers might enter mentoring relationships expecting that mentors will provide them with all of the opportunities the protégé seeks.

  ▶ Workers might enter an experience thinking that the employer will pay for it, but the employer expects workers to file certain reports before reimbursing them for their participation.

When training and development professionals clarify the work involved in a particular activity and the responsibilties for performing it, these issues are less likely to arise. More important, clarifying expectations of learning activities might help workers realize that they hold primary responsibility for their learning.

6. When Designing Materials That Workers Might Use for Informal Learning, Design for "Learn-Ability"

As Marsick and Watkins (1990) noted, many workers initiate informal learning activities to solve an immediate problem. In doing so, they often consult references, reports, policies and procedures guides, and similar materials. One of the ways in which training and development professionals can support informal learning is by making sure that such materials are designed for "learn-ability."

Designing published materials for learn-ability involves designing materials for physical, intellectual, and emotional access (Carliner, 2000). Physical access refers to the ease with which workers can find the information they seek. Training and development professionals can facilitate physical access to information by

▶ Providing "findability aids," devices that help workers easily locate documents of interest. For online searches, that involves indexing documents with clear and widely understood keywords. Clear filing systems help workers find print materials and online materials that are not indexed.

▶ Starting materials with clear opening paragraphs. Because workers tend to read work-related documents the same way they read news stories—that is, they read the first paragraph to determine whether to continue reading—write clear opening paragraphs that state the "who, what, where, when, and why" of the document.

▶ Using identical formats to present identical information. For example, specific policies and procedures might follow an identical structure that starts with the presentation of the policy, then outlines the procedure for administering it, and closes with questions and answers about eligibility and how to handle special cases. Once workers become used to such a format, they use it to search for information when reading about new policies. For example, suppose Julie heard that her company offers a tuition reimbursement program and would like to find out whether she's eligible; she would immediately turn to the first part of the question-and-answer section, which describes eligibility criteria.

▶ Providing tools to direct workers to segments of interest within documents. One of the most common tools is section headings. In online documents, *breadcrumbs* let users see where they are within a larger website, and a list of links on a page (like a miniature table of contents) lets users easily jump to parts on that same page. In printed documents, tables of contents, page numbers, indexes, and running headers or footers help workers easily jump to pages of interest.

▶ Providing an indication of progress through the document such as completion bars on tutorials to tell workers how much they have finished, which workers find helpful.

Training and development professionals can also facilitate intellectual access, which refers to how easy the materials are to understand. Specific issues to consider include

▶ Clarity. Does the document use familiar terminology and fully explain all concepts, so that workers can comprehend material on the first read, without having to read and reread passages several times?

▶ Completeness. Does the document provide all of the information needed to apply the content on the job? For example, if the document explains a process, does it list the criteria for successful completion and suggest how to handle common errors that arise in the process?

- ▸ Application. Does the document provide examples, illustrations, exercises, case studies, and similar resources to help workers visualize how they might use the guidelines, policies, procedures, processes, and other materials described in the documents in their environments?

Emotional access refers to workers' emotional responses to the messages in the learning materials. Do the content, terminology, and examples reflect the environment in which readers work? If not, the workers might have difficulty seeing the relevance. Similarly, if the content describes changes in processes and procedures, does it acknowledge the possible apprehensive feelings of workers about these changes?

7. Provide Tutoring and Coaching Throughout the Process

In support of informal learning efforts, training and development professionals also need to provide private coaching and tutoring that workers feel comfortable requesting and using. This type of tutoring and coaching occurs in addition to coaching provided to help workers clarify their goals and choose learning activities. Specifically, this type of coaching and tutoring provides assistance with

- ▸ technical content with which workers have difficulty, such as statistics or a particular type of strategic thinking
- ▸ technology, by helping workers work past technical difficulties that arise when learning informally, such as an application that unexpectedly crashes
- ▸ follow-up, to ensure that workers are following the learning paths they identified, or to determine why they chose not to
- ▸ feedback, which helps workers assess their progress on their learning paths and correct any knowledge learned incorrectly.

8. Guide Facilitation of Nonlearning Situations to Encourage Learning

Much informal learning happens through group processes, such as meetings, collaborating on work projects, and brainstorming. But such activities rarely have learning as their primary purpose, so the learning often happens unconsciously.

Training and development professionals can encourage the use of these specific practices to help identify learning when it occurs in these situations:

- ▸ Using a brainstorming approach so that workers can hear the diversity of opinions in the room and let that diversity influence their own opinions.

Such a process works best when all workers have a stake in the work. Note that the facilitator needs to provide each person with an opportunity to participate and prevent one group or individual from dominating the conversation.

▶ At the ends of meetings, asking participants to reflect on what they learned. This helps to surface any learning that occurred unconsciously.

9. Help Workers Recognize What They Have Learned Informally

Helping workers recognize that learning has occurred is an important means of supporting the informal learning process. It helps workers and managers acknowledge the new skills, knowledge, and experience, and build their trust in informal learning processes. Recognizing insights learned and skills developed informally involves making tacit knowledge explicit.

Questioning is at the heart of this step. The questioning process is intended as a means of helping workers clarify what was learned—it is not intended as an interrogation. One technique uses a series of questions to help workers identify what they have learned and how it has affected them (Marsick and Watkins, 2011). Here are some guidelines:

1. Begin with factual questions that explore the "whats" of learning, such as surface facts, observable data, quotes, and common knowledge gained.
2. Follow up with reflective questions that explore emotional reactions to learning.
3. Continue questioning with interpretive questions that explore the significance and implications of the learning to workers and how they plan to respond to it.
4. Conclude with questions about how the learning might affect future decisions. This leads to strategic insights about the learning.

Another technique for unlocking the learning that has occurred in everyday work processes involves asking workers about what happened and who was involved at key milestones in those processes. This questioning usually elicits detailed responses into which are embedded insights about lessons learned implicitly through the job.

Training and development professionals can support this process of eliciting learning by preparing discussion guides that suggest ways in which managers and senior workers might handle these conversations with workers. Discussion guides identify different reasons that coaches might interact with workers and suggest questions to ask in particular situations so that coaches effectively elicit the lessons learned through informal learning.

10. Encourage Personal and Formal Acknowledgment of Informal Learning Efforts

Conscious or not, informal learning is often a solitary activity. Sometimes for the lack of consciousness by the worker, sometimes for the lack of awareness of others, the learning goes unacknowledged.

Workers who are motivated by external recognition value a formal acknowledgment by a manager that he or she is aware of the worker's participation in informal learning efforts. This acknowledgment can encourage workers to continue their self-directed learning activities. For the most part, acknowledgment of informal learning can consist of a simple comment like "Hey, I notice that you learned something" when someone is seen applying a new technique on the job, or "I saw you participated in this activity" in response to seeing a worker's name on a report of participation in a lunch-and-learn session or similar event.

More formal recognition might involve invitations to apply a worker's newly gained expertise, such as invitations to serve on task forces or consult on high-profile projects, and appointments to advisory positions. Promotion or a lateral transfer into a position that has greater capabilities for a promotion also provide recognition for skills and knowledge acquired informally.

Think About This

Although supporting informal learning involves many institutionalized programs, these programs are merely intended to focus on and strengthen learning processes that already occur within the organization.

Getting It Done

Use Worksheets 4–1 and 4–2 to help guide efforts to support informal learning in your organization.

Worksheet 4–1. Checklist of Support for Informal Learning

Use the following checklist to make sure that your organization has the support in place to leverage the informal learning that occurs there.

A. Does your organization offer a framework for informal learning?

☐ Have you set clear expectations about informal learning so stakeholders have realistic goals for it and recognize what it can and cannot accomplish?

☐ Have you gained executive support for informal learning efforts through official statements of support, funding, use of work time for informal learning, and their active participation in it?

☐ Does your organization have an internal infrastructure of content that workers can leverage for informal learning including policies, procedures and processes, guidelines, standards, marketing literature about current products, user documents about current products, service documents about current products, planning documents about future products, service records, and customer records?

☐ Have you secured external content to extend the opportunities for informal learning, including courses developed outside the organization, bibliographic databases, and subscriptions to periodicals?

☐ Do you continually promote the availability of resources for informal learning so workers are always aware it is available?

☐ Do you emphasize ongoing learning through performance planning and evaluation, regular skills assessments, and career planning?

☐ Does your organization maintain content so that workers always have access to current material?

B. Does your organization support individual workers with their informal learning efforts?

☐ Do workers have access to someone who can help them clarify their learning goals and the paths toward those goals?

☐ Do workers have access to someone who can help them develop independent study and research skills so they can find material on their own and, when they do, identify its strengths and weaknesses as a source of data on which to base decisions?

☐ Does the organization promote collaborative working skills so workers are open to learning from one another?

☐ Do workers have access to someone who can help them set realistic expectations for informal learning efforts so that they are aware of their responsibilities in the learning process?

☐ Do people in the organization design materials for "learn-ability" so workers might use these materials for informal learning? More specifically, do people design materials to ensure that readers can find, understand, and appropriately respond to informal learning content?

☐ Does the organization provide access to tutoring and coaching throughout the process so that confusion does not cause a setback in learning? So that workers feel encouraged to finish their learning efforts?

☐ Do workers have access to someone who can help them recognize what they have learned informally so workers can integrate that content into their work?

☐ Do managers personally acknowledge informal learning efforts so workers do not feel anonymous in their informal learning?

☐ Does the organization offer ways to formally acknowledge learning so workers can tangibly benefit from their expanded body of skills and knowledge?

Worksheet 4–2. Supporting Informal Learning in Your Organization

1. After speaking with Curtis about his experiences at his previous corporation, the human resources manager in the new general contracting organization where Curtis now works has decided that all managers should have mobile access to policies and procedures, so that they can fully understand those policies when faced with an on-the-spot decision like the one that Curtis faced when dealing with the employee in his previous job (which resulted in Curtis firing the worker on the spot, based on his incomplete understanding of the policies).

   Specifically, what types of support issues should this human resources manager consider when implementing this plan to provide availability of policies and procedures on smartphones and mobile devices?

   _____

   _____

   _____

   _____

   _____

Debriefing of exercise 1. Certainly providing workers with access to the policies and procedures can offer great convenience—but only when offered with related support. Consider these issues. First, as basic as this might seem, the human resources manager should make sure that managers carry smartphones or similar mobile devices to work sites and that they also have Internet access there. If not, a great concept will go nowhere for lack of equipment.

   Second, the human resources manager also needs to regularly promote this mobile access, so field managers realize that, even in the field, they can check the online policies guide when questions arise. Third, because interpretations are often needed when applying policies to specific cases, field managers also need access to someone in the main office who might help them interpret challenging situations.

2. Marley would like to join a professional organization for business-to-business marketing professionals. One of the reasons that Marley hopes to join the organization is for the networking opportunities. But one of the other reasons is for the learning opportunities. Among the benefits of membership is access to a database of business publications that she might not otherwise have access to. Marley is requesting that her employer cover the membership costs, because it can assist her in her current job as well as prepare her for a future one.

Should the employer cover the cost? Why do you feel this way?

_____

_____

_____

_____

_____

Debriefing of exercise 2. The cost of memberships always poses a challenge to organizations. Some have a policy of supporting a certain number of memberships per worker. Some have a designated member who is supposed to share materials and lessons learned with the rest of the staff.

Some purchase several memberships, partly as a perk for workers but also partly in the hope that workers might take advantage of the resources. And some organizations have a policy of shared burden; because the membership provides long-term benefits to the worker, the organization pays for part of it and the worker pays the rest.

Because memberships in professional organizations provide educational resources through meetings, webinars, magazine subscriptions, and access to members-only reports, however, organizations should seriously consider supporting memberships as a means of making informal learning activities and content available to workers.

5

Group Activities That Promote Informal Learning

What's Inside This Chapter

In this chapter, you'll learn about

▶ the social nature of informal learning
▶ ways that people learn informally through others, at events and during interactions with other workers.

Unlike the first four chapters of this book, the next several chapters combine the elements of a text and a reference. The first sections of these chapters briefly introduce concepts; the later sections describe specific ways to apply the concepts. You might review the later sections briefly now, then refer back to them later, when you plan to use a particular type of informal learning.

The Social Nature of Learning

To consider informal learning in groups, think back to Curtis and Marley. Both had interactions that helped them learn informally on the job:

▶ Curtis, the site supervisor for a construction firm, lost his first supervisory position because he fired a worker without authorization. When the situation arose that led Curtis to fire the worker, he remembered something that one of his colleagues had mentioned during an off-site managers' meeting: Managers had a responsibility to deal effectively with safety violations, especially when the employee is at fault. This message led Curtis to misinterpret the company policy.

▶ Marley, the once-unfocused junior account executive with an advertising agency, became an expert in business-to-business sales through the guidance of her mentor. Through a series of discussions and "what if" situations, her mentor helped her recognize her lack of focus and hone her skills in landing business-to-business advertising accounts.

Learning in both of these instances resulted from interactions with others: In Curtis's case, with his colleagues in a meeting, and in Marley's case, through ongoing conversations with her increasingly trusted mentor.

Social Learning: A Phenomenon Rooted in a Philosophy of Learning

As noted in chapter 2, some definitions of *learning* describe it as a change in behavior. In such instances, learners succeed when they adopt the behaviors defined in the learning objectives. Training and development professionals write these objectives and state them in terms that are observable and measurable so that they can track the extent to which learning has occurred. But not all learning happens according to a script. Learning can also be influenced by the cultural environment of the workplace and the personal values each worker brings to it. Consider Curtis again. Although he works as a construction manager during the day, he also owns and works a hobby farm. Because he owns the farm he does not need permission to implement his decisions and can resolve issues immediately as he sees fit. That is the context for his feeling empowered to fire a worker who repeatedly flaunted the safety rules. A training and development professional could not have been aware of this background, but it affects how the worker integrates knowledge all the same.

Similarly, Marley had difficulty focusing in her job because her business degree curriculum had overwhelmingly focused on consumer advertising. Although her employer had some consumer accounts, the majority of work came from business-to-business accounts. So previous learning experiences unintentionally favored consumer over business-to-business accounts and, faced with the mixed message of the lessons she learned before joining the firm and those learned afterward, Marley had difficulty focusing.

These two examples illustrate how workers construct their base of knowledge through social interactions—some inside the workplace, some outside of it. Some educational philosophers believe that the behaviorist and the pure cognitivist approaches to learning (described in chapters 1 and 2) overlook these social and situational influences. They propose *constructivist learning,* which acknowledges these influences and suggests that instructors promote learning through social interactions and powerful experiences.

This *constructivist* approach to learning underlies much informal learning, especially learning under learner control. Training and development professionals can *anticipate* outcomes from a constructivist learning approach, but not necessarily *predict* them, as they can in behaviorist or cognitivist approaches to learning. One of the resulting challenges to training and development professionals is identifying the types of group interactions that facilitate learning, anticipating what types of positive and negative lessons workers might learn from those interactions, and influencing those interactions when possible to promote learning—whatever form the outcome ultimately takes.

Basic Rule

One of the most powerful ways that workers learn informally is through their interactions with others. The lessons learned range from tips that enhance performance on the job to insights that shape attitudes and values about the workplace and life outside of it.

Two general sets of group interactions promote learning in collaboration with others:

> ▶ Events, which refer to formally scheduled activities. Specific types of events include formal courses, lunch and learns, meetings seminars and symposia, conferences, and webinars.
> ▶ Interactions with others, through either formally structured groups and projects or loosely structured networks. Specific types of interactions with others include coaching, communities, mentoring, networks, peer learning, and work assignments and projects.

Many of these types of group interactions already exist in organizations. Informal learning tends to work most effectively when it leverages existing opportunities rather than creating new ones. When promoting informal learning in collaboration with others, pay attention to the following conditions and suggestions for success:

- ▶ Match the learning opportunity with the appropriate phase in the life cycle of a job.
- ▶ Help participants in an activity recognize its potential for learning.
- ▶ Make sure that participants have the resources they need to learn when engaged in that activity; this might involve preparing materials to accompany the activity.
- ▶ Provide participants with tools for identifying lessons learned and transferring them to the job.

The next two sections describe several specific types of events and interactions with others that offer informal learning opportunities. The lists are not exhaustive but provide an overview of the most common opportunities and ways that you can leverage them for informal learning.

Events That Support Informal Learning

The following sections describe four specific types of events that contribute to informal learning, suggest when and how you might use them, and how they adjust the levers of informal learning.

Formal Courses

As ironic as this might sound, formal courses provide informal learning experiences because they can help workers achieve personal learning objectives or address developmental needs. Formal courses are also *synchronous*, meaning that the instructor and learners all participate at the same time. So participants have the opportunity to interact with other participants and, in the process, experience additional learning opportunities to those named in the course description. Typically, these types of formal courses support informal learning:

- ▶ training courses offered by employers, professional associations, and trade associations
- ▶ programs offered outside of a formal training program and often not offering any credit, such as
  - ▶ continuing education programs offered by public schools, colleges, and universities
  - ▶ courses offered by museums, health-related organizations, and other community organizations.

Success with integrating formal courses into an informal learning program depends on participants' abilities to link the formal classroom learning to their personal informal learning agendas. This requires excellent synthesis skills—the ability to see connections in material that, at first glance, might not have a relationship.

Training and development professionals can support informal learning through formal courses by advising workers when a formal course might help them meet a personal learning goal (especially one offered outside the organization) and by suggesting how the course helps meet these goals if workers do not see the connection.

Training and development professionals can also advocate for organizational support for participation in these courses, either by providing work time to learn, funds, or both. When support is not provided and workers would significantly benefit from the learning experience, training and development professionals might encourage workers to invest their own resources in these courses. Figure 5–1 suggests how formal courses adjust the levers of informal learning.

Figure 5–1. How Formal Courses Contribute to Informal Learning

Informal ⟋ Formal	Informal ⟋ Formal	Informal ⟋ Formal	Informal ⟋ Formal	Informal ⟋ Formal
Process	**Location**	**Purpose**	**Content**	**Consciousness**
Instructors and administrators typically control the learning process.	Formal courses, especially classroom courses, occur in classrooms, meeting rooms, and similar places intended for learning.	Although the primary purpose of formal courses is learning, participants who have an informal agenda might see the formal agenda as secondary to their purposes.	Content varies, from abstract to technical, related to a practical, everyday skill.	Although participants will likely be conscious of learning the formal objectives, they may or may not be fully conscious of learning that occurs in groups and activities.

Lunch and Learns

"Lunch and learn" refers to an event of 90 minutes or less that occurs over a meal (typically lunch, hence the name) and during which participants discuss technical or developmental content. For example, an HR department might plan an event to discuss balancing work and personal lives—and might provide sandwiches and beverages to encourage workers to attend.

Although lunch-and-learn sessions rarely have formal learning objectives, they usually have a tight focus on a single topic and are kept brief. A designated organizer invites speakers and participants, coaches speakers to provide meaningful content to participants, introduces the speakers at the event, suggests ways workers can apply the content in their jobs, and thanks speakers and participants afterward. Training and development professionals are usually the designated organizer and facilitator of these events. They can further support informal learning through lunch and learns by linking the topic of a session with the goals and interests of participants and by suggesting ways that workers can continue their exploration of the topic back on the job. Figure 5–2 suggests how lunch and learns adjust the levers of informal learning.

Figure 5–2. How Lunch and Learns Contribute to Informal Learning

Process	Location	Purpose	Content	Consciousness
Agendas for lunch and learns are usually coordinated by a facilitator and are often driven by that person.	Although lunch and learns usually occur in a meeting room or classroom (traditional or virtual), they can really occur anywhere, such as a corner of a cafeteria or a coffeehouse.	Learning is usually the primary purpose of the event, but networking and team relationships often serve a strong secondary purpose.	Content varies, from abstract to technical, related to a practical, everyday skill. The nature of the content varies by common characteristic of the participants.	Although participants will likely be conscious of learning the formal objectives, they may or may not be fully conscious of learning that occurs in groups and activities.

Meetings

Although people rarely call meetings for the specific purpose of learning, many workers find meetings to be one of the most important means of learning because participants share and discuss key information about current assignments. Effective meetings usually start with a clearly defined purpose and have a formal agenda that participants can expect to cover in the given time. Effective meetings are also announced well in advance, provide participants with reminders about the meetings, and are appropriately documented. *Appropriate* documentation refers to notes (sometimes called *minutes*) that record decisions made, key information shared, responsibilities assigned, and dates when those people must report back on their responsibilities. Most importantly, effective meetings have leaders who take responsibility for each of these issues.

Training and development professionals can support meetings as learning opportunities in several ways. They can provide guidance to meeting leaders so that meetings run efficiently and stay on topic and workers feel motivated to participate in meetings. Training and development professionals can also provide job aids that help meeting leaders establish agendas and record notes, and they can coach meeting leaders on ways to keep meetings focused, while allowing for exploration of unanticipated but important points of learning that may arise. For example, training and development professionals might suggest ending each meeting with a discussion of lessons learned or a debriefing of the meeting process. Figure 5–3 suggests how meetings specifically adjust the levers of informal learning.

Figure 5–3. How Meetings Contribute to Informal Learning

Process	Location	Purpose	Content	Consciousness
Informal — Formal	Informal — Formal	Informal — Formal	Informal — Formal	Informal — Formal
On the one hand, effective meetings have facilitators. On the other hand, facilitators focus on achieving the meeting agenda, not learning objectives.	Many meetings occur in places intended for learning, but many others occur in places intended for socializing.	Learning is a secondary objective of most meetings.	Although much meeting content is technical, much learning content is developmental.	Although participants expect to learn about the technical content related to the purpose of the meeting, much of the actual learning is unconscious.

Seminars, Symposia, Conferences, and Webinars

Seminars, symposia, conferences, and webinars are special types of meetings that let participants explore one or more topics of interest. Most of these events have facilitators. Organizations often sponsor these events to update the knowledge and skills of current staff members and business partners (such as suppliers and customers). Organizations prefer these events because they are often shorter than a full training course, let participants tailor an agenda to their own needs and interests, or let participants consider a topic in depth.

Each of these events has a particular style and focus:

▶ Seminars (sometimes called *lectures*) are usually one- to three-hour events that explore one topic in depth. Seminars typically include one or more guest speakers who share knowledge and spark thought, and they often include interaction between the audience and speaker and among members of the audience.

▶ Symposia have a single focus, but it is usually broader than that of a seminar and explored from a variety of perspectives. Most symposia only have one event running at a time and might last from one to several days. Most symposia also include related events, such as meals and receptions, for participants to casually interact with—and learn from—one another.

▶ Conferences are about the same length as symposia, but usually have a broader focus and schedule several simultaneous events. Like symposia, conferences include less structured events for participants to casually interact with—and learn from—one another.

▶ Although webinars get their name by combining *web* with *seminar*, webinars have come to refer to seminars, symposia, and conferences held online.

Although seminars, symposia, and conferences are all formally scheduled events, many training and development professionals consider them forms of informal learning.

The success of these events depends on two general factors. The first is prepared speakers who address topics of interest to participants—in ways that engage the participants, through clear, succinct messages, well-designed slides, and similar visual aids.

The other key characteristic of successful seminars, symposia, conferences, and webinars is having plenty of opportunities for participants to learn from one another (called *peer learning)*. This involves ensuring that speakers lead participants in interactive activities (more than merely leaving time at the end of a presentation for participants to ask questions). Such facilitated activities ensure that all participants are engaged. Training and development professionals often need to coach speakers to effectively present material and engage their audiences.

In addition to planning these events so that they promote various types of learning, training and development professionals can provide support for seminars, symposia, and conferences by advising workers about upcoming events of interest and encouraging them to participate. Training and development professionals can also advocate for organizations to support workers' participation in these events and provide resources that help workers reflect on their learning after the event. Figure 5–4 suggests how seminars, symposia, conferences, and webinars adjust the levers of informal learning.

Figure 5–4. How Seminars, Symposia, Conferences, and Webinars Contribute to Informal Learning

Process	Location	Purpose	Content	Consciousness
The event and its agenda are formally structured by the planners of the event. But because the scheduled sessions and social events let participants interact with speakers, participants control part of their agendas.	The presentations at these events usually occur in spaces intended for learning (such as meeting rooms and classrooms). But these events usually include social events in other places. For example, one year, ASTD held an event for one of its conferences at Universal Studios in Orlando.	Learning is a primary purpose of these events.	The planners of these events and speakers determine the content that is formally presented; discussion points from the participants steer the learning in other directions.	Participants are concious of learning related to the stated goals of the event, and some, though not all, of the learning occurs through interactions with speakers and other participants.

Interactions With Others That Promote Informal Learning

Planned and unplanned interactions with others are the second of two categories of opportunities that promote or support informal learning in the workplace. The following sections explore six types of interactions with others that contribute to informal learning.

Coaching

The term "coaching" refers to formal efforts to provide workers with feedback on their performance of a particular task or job and, if needed, suggestions on how to improve that performance. Coaching relationships typically involve two parties: workers, who perform a job or task, and coaches, who provide the feedback and suggestions. This individualized, tailored feedback can provide workers with unusually deep insights rooted in a particular situation (a teachable moment) and linked to their own knowledge and experience.

Using Technology in Coaching Efforts

Technology helps organizations provide workers with feedback on their performance. In certain environments, such as manufacturing and telemarketing, technology tracks the amount of work performed, the time needed to perform it, the number of errors, and similar types of information. This type of feedback provides workers with quantitative feedback on their performance. Project management systems provide project teams with similar types of feedback on development projects. More sophisticated technology can provide intelligent tutoring—anticipating questions and providing responses based on what task the user is performing at a given moment. For example, some language-learning websites let learners practice conversations, but the conversations occur between the learner and the computer. The computer chooses responses based on the words of the learner.

Software that allows people to communicate with one another also provides a means of sharing feedback, even when the workers involved do not sit near one another. For example, many professional, certified coaches have clients who live beyond the metropolitan area in which the coach lives. These coaches typically interact with workers through telephones and virtual meeting software.

Training and development professionals can support coaching by raising awareness among managers and others that they serve a coaching role; many of these people have limited awareness of, or comfort with, this role. They can also provide managers and others who serve in a coaching role with guidance in how to coach, focusing on the types of issues to raise—and the ones to let go—and how to effectively provide feedback. Figure 5–5 suggests how coaching adjusts the levers of informal learning.

Figure 5–5. How Coaching Contributes to Informal Learning

Process	Location	Purpose	Content	Consciousness
Informal — Formal	Informal — Formal	Informal — Formal	Informal — Formal	Informal — Formal
Coaching is initiated by observations of performance in the workplace, or by a request from a worker for guidance in improving performance. External coaches explicitly ask workers to drive the coaching process.	Coaching occurs in the workplace, a private office or meeting room, or some similar location not exclusively intended for learning.	Coaching in the context of a specific job tells workers how their performance can more closely match standards established by the organiza-tion. Other types of coaching often assists with similar goals.	The organiza-tion establishes the standards against which coaches assess performance in immediate jobs. For longer term coaching, the focus is more developmental.	Workers are usually conscious that they are learning.

Communities

Communities refer to groups of people who share a professional interest or background and discuss opportunities, challenges, and feelings related to it. Communities can meet in person or online (or a combination of the two).

Clubs, chambers of commerce, professional associations, and affinity groups (people who share a common demographic characteristic or interest) are typical examples of professional communities that meet in person. Most of these groups meet on a regular basis—weekly, monthly, or quarterly—and build their regular meetings around a meal, guest speaker, or social event. An ASTD chapter is an example of such a community.

Online communities bring together people online who might not otherwise have the opportunity to interact. For example, the website LinkedIn lets professionals build communities with people outside of their organizations and professions, and lets members form "groups" to discuss common interests. Online communities typically exist in one of these formats:

- ▶ Listservs, communities in which people interact through email messages. Participants formally register with a listserv and then receive messages sent by other members of the community and reply to those messages. Listservs are among the earliest forms of online communities.
- ▶ Message boards, also called *forums*, in which people visit a website, read comments posted by members of the community, and post responses to those comments. Message boards are key components of many learning management systems (like Plateau) and course management systems (like Blackboard and Moodle). Some message boards restrict membership; others are open to anyone.
- ▶ Discussion groups, which are similar to message boards, but are integrated into social networking sites like Facebook and LinkedIn, and often have easier-to-use interfaces than message boards.

Training and development professionals can support communities by establishing them and inviting eligible workers to participate, planning the first events (if any) and "seeding" discussions during crucial early months. But as many learn through experience, the majority of the support effort needed for a community occurs after it is initially established. Keeping the conversation going in the long term requires sustained attention to the community, ongoing assessment of the needs and interests of community members, and providing information and programming that meets those needs.

Although volunteers assume these responsibilities in some communities, in many others, volunteers do not rise to the task. So in some communities, training and development professionals fill these gaps and monitor discussions among members of the community to make sure that the discussions follow guidelines established for the community and users respect the integrity of each community member. Research—like the early work of Lee Sproull and Sara Kiesler (1991)—suggests that online contributors are often less sensitive to etiquette than they are in person. Figure 5–6 suggests how communities adjust the levers of informal learning.

Figure 5–6. How Communities Contribute to Informal Learning

Process	Location	Purpose	Content	Consciousness
Informal — Formal	Informal — Formal	Informal — Formal	Informal — Formal	Informal — Formal
When one exists, a moderator (or similar leader) generally oversees the learning process. Otherwise, participants generally control the learning process themselves.	Whether in person or online, participants expect, at the least, an exchange of information and, at the most, some structured learning. Many in-person meetings occur in meeting rooms and classrooms.	Learning is both a primary and secondary goal of communities.	In some instances, the learning is intended to focus on the technical (as in a community of information technology professionals); in other instances, it is developmental (such as career advancement tips shared in a conversation of an affinity group). Furthermore, both the moderator (if one exists) and participants drive the learning agenda.	Participants usually join communities expecting to learn something, though they often do not know what they expect to learn.

Mentoring

Mentoring refers to a relationship between a *mentor*—someone with experience who "provides advice, guidance, support, and feedback" (Driscoll and Carliner, 2005, p. 188)—and a *protégé,* someone who wants to learn from the experience of the mentor. Mentoring relationships "facilitate personal and professional growth, and . . . foster career development" (Driscoll and Carliner, p. 188).

Mentoring contrasts with coaching in that mentoring is often provided outside the context of a job, is intended for the personal development of the protégé, and has no formal agenda unless the protégé suggests one. In contrast, coaching is usually provided within the context of a particular job with the intention of improving performance in that job.

Mentoring relationships nurture workers in a variety of ways, including these:

► Mentors help protégés develop strategies for advancing their careers and for addressing immediate challenges in their workplaces. For example, a mentor might advise a protégé about developmental opportunities that might benefit the protégé for a future career opportunity. Mentors might also introduce protégés to their contacts.

► Mentors collaborate with protégés on work projects. Regardless of whether the mentor or the protégé initiates the project, the protégé typically apprentices with the mentor.

► Mentors serve as role models; protégés use the examples of their mentors in establishing career goals and charting career paths.

Although mentoring tends to focus on the development of the protégé, it also serves as a powerful learning experience for the mentor. Many mentors note that, in addition to valued relationships, they develop coaching and leadership skills through mentoring. Sometimes the protégé helps the mentor develop skills, which is called *reverse mentoring*. (This arrangement works especially well with technology, with which younger protégés tend to have higher comfort levels.) Mentoring can happen in person or online. Software that operates like online dating software can match mentors and protégés who might not have met otherwise. The relationship continues thorough email, social networking, Skype, and similar types of software.

Mentoring can occur formally or informally. Informal mentoring often results from chance meetings or prior connections. Formal mentoring results from the efforts of an employer or some similar organization to establish a mentoring program. Many of these programs merely involve matching potential mentors and protégés. Ideally the match is based on shared interests or characteristics, but the match sometimes results from the willingness of a person to serve as a mentor to someone else. As a result, formally established mentoring relationships often have disappointing results.

Training and development professionals can support mentoring by facilitating the match of potential mentors with protégés and by helping set the expectations of both parties at the beginning of the relationship so both have realistic expectations of it. In addition, training and development professionals can support mentoring by acting as a mediator if problems arise in the relationships between mentors and protégés. Figure 5–7 suggests how mentoring adjust the levers of informal learning.

Figure 5–7. How Mentoring Contributes to Informal Learning

Process	Location	Purpose	Content	Consciousness
The mentoring process is generally controlled by the learner.	Mentoring typically occurs in social settings, for example, in restaurants, coffeehouses, or offices, or through telephone or online chats.	Mentoring serves both learning and developmental purposes.	Typical mentoring focuses on developmental issues, but occasionally addresses technical and everyday issues.	In some instances, participants are conscious that learning is occuring; in others, they only realize much later that learning has occurred.

Networks

Networks refer to the complex web of people whom a worker contacts when questions arise and he or she is looking for information and advice on work- or career-related topics. With the rise of social media such as blogs, Facebook, LinkedIn, social bookmarking tools, and Twitter, these networks increasingly include people from outside the geographic community.

Some have dubbed these online networks as *personal learning networks*. Blogger Kate Klingensmith (2009) defined them as "the entire collection of people with whom you engage and exchange information, usually online. Personal Learning Networks, or PLNs, have been around forever. Originally, they were your family and friends, maybe other educators you worked with, but as the Internet and web 2.0 tools have become nearly ubiquitous, PLNs can include tons of different communities—social networking sites like Facebook, blogs, Twitter, wikis, social bookmarking tools, LinkedIn, and so many more."

Although most current writing focuses on the role of technology in building and supporting networks, some of the most significant factors in building and nurturing them are interpersonal processes. Workers need to feel comfortable contacting people when questions arise. Comfort levels vary with perceptions of authority (or lack of authority) and personality differences (introversion or extroversion). Similarly, members of the network must have a general respect for one another, or they may dismiss comments from other members.

Networks primarily contribute to informal learning in these ways:

  ▶ offering immediate answers to pressing questions
  ▶ inspiring new perspectives on, and ideas about, a subject, either by broadening the scope of a subject or by adding depth to the understanding of it
  ▶ suggesting new topics about which to learn
  ▶ modeling behavior for interacting in communities; by observing the behavior of others in the network, workers get a sense of both dos and don'ts for interacting in professional and organizational settings.

Training and development professionals can support the formation of networks in much the same way that they promote communities. In addition, they can encourage workers to include people in their networks who do not work for their organization, so that workers have access to the broadest possible base of knowledge and experiences—and ensure that organizations support workers in networking outside their organizations (a concern in some organizations). Training and development professionals have the option, too, of playing "matchmaker," suggesting people that workers might include in their networks. Figure 5–8 suggests how networks adjust the levers of informal learning.

Peer Learning

Peer learning refers to a class of activities in which people who share a status in the organization or community work together to develop their knowledge, skills, and attitudes from interactions with each other.

Figure 5–8. How Networks Contribute to Informal Learning

Process	Location	Purpose	Content	Consciousness
Networks are generally not controlled by the learner or, at most, minimally controlled.	Networking typically occurs in social settings or online.	Networking serves both learning and developmental purposes.	Typical networking primarily focuses on developmental needs but can also address technical and everyday issues.	In some instances, participants are conscious that learning has occurred; in other instances, they only realize much later that learning has occurred.

Peer learning takes several forms. One of the best known is the book group, in which people who share the status of interested readers all read the same book and then meet to discuss it. Although most people consider book groups to be a social activity, some workplaces have formal and informal groups whose primary purpose is sharing and reading books. Another of the best known forms of peer learning is the water cooler conversation, in which co-workers share valuable information during an impromptu gathering in the office.

Although peer learning has a long tradition in face-to-face formats, online communication has transformed the experience. Social networking applications provide peers who would not otherwise meet with the opportunity to interact. Before online communication, factors such as geography and location in the organizational hierarchy would have prevented these people from interacting with—and learning from—one another. Unlike the formal groups on social networking applications, peer learning opportunities often result from contact initiated by an individual—such as one LinkedIn member contacting three or four others to establish a short-term group to study a project. The discussion would continue over email, in a meeting (virtual or in person), or with the exchange of documents.

Although peer learning groups need not have formal learning objectives, having a well-defined purpose helps the group decide which activities they will choose to pursue and which ones they will not. The success of peer groups depends on a number of factors, including access to expertise and resources and a willingness to engage in honest conversation and dialogue.

Strong group processes, too, are essential to the success of peer learning. Because team members learn from one another, the group processes need to provide everyone an equal opportunity to speak and promote respect for all opinions expressed.

Training and development professionals support peer learning by promoting all types of work-related interactions among co-workers and by helping workers realize what they might have learned through these interactions. Training and development professionals also need to advocate for peer learning with senior management, making them aware that conversations around the water cooler might start with discussions of the latest sports event or *American Idol* episode, but often meander to work-related topics and to resolutions of problems and improvement of productivity. Figure 5–9 suggests how peer learning adjusts the levers of informal learning.

Figure 5–9. How Peer Learning Contributes to Informal Learning

Process	Location	Purpose	Content	Consciousness
Participants control all aspects of their learning process.	Participants can choose where they meet to learn. Some might choose less formal settings, like cubicles, coffeeshops, or restaurants, while others tend to choose meeting rooms and classrooms.	Learning groups have learning as a primary focus. In many instances, however, the learning on the agenda (such as a particular book) often differs from the deep learning that occurs (such as insights into one another and interacting with people).	The nature of the content varies widely, depending on the specific agenda of the group, as well as the nature of the discussions. But even formally established goals range from technical to developmental content.	In terms of the stated reasons for the peer group, learning tends to occur consciously. But as noted earlier, much unexpected learning occurs, and that often happens unconsciously.

Work Assignments and Projects

Work assignments and projects refer to situations in which informal learning occurs through the process of workers performing their jobs. These assignments and projects often provide some of the most significant learning opportunities because workers learn and do simultaneously. In fact, others who have written about informal learning, such as Marilyn Laiken and her colleagues at the University of Toronto, often focus on this incidental learning that occurs within the context of people performing their jobs.

Several factors make work assignments and projects valuable learning experiences. One is that the lessons learned have immediate relevance to a particular work project. Another is the institutional history that some team members offer to the individual or work group—history that might not otherwise be available and puts immediate work into a larger context.

Although learning through work assignments and projects can offer positive, indeed transformational, learning experiences, the learning can just as easily result from a combination of less-than-satisfying work experiences. Benign neglect by one group of workers—such as failing to document a change in a procedure—can result in unexpected learning by another group of workers. The latter group of workers might feel that the experience that caused rework could have been avoided.

One of the primary ways that training and development professionals can support learning through work assignments and projects is by helping workers realize that learning has occurred and identifying what they have learned. Researcher Victoria Marsick refers to this as "surfacing" unconscious learning. Typically, managers and co-workers have the responsibility for "surfacing" this learning, but training and development professionals can further these efforts by providing managers and co-workers with interview scripts and other means of eliciting learning. Figure 5–10 suggests how team work assignments and projects adjust the levers of informal learning.

Figure 5–10. How Work Assignments and Projects Contribute to Informal Learning

Process	Location	Purpose	Content	Consciousness
Although much of the learning is unconscious, to the extent that any control exists over learning, learners control their own.	Learning occurs in the workplace.	Learning is a secondary purpose of most work assignments and projects, except for assignments specifically identified as developmental, such as apprenticeships, internships, and training rotations.	Workers learn all types of content through work assignments and projects. In some instances, they develop and hone technical skills related to the work. In other instances, workers learn more abstract content, such as concepts guiding the work and how to finesse challenging situations.	When workers are primarily focused on the work at hand, many do not realize that any learning has occurred.

A Note About Group Activities and Informal Learning

Each type of event and interaction with others described in this chapter contributes to informal learning. As presented in the figures showing the levers of learning, however, these types of informal learning require shared responsibilities for, and participation in, learning between workers and their organizations. Workers are not left on their own to learn.

Because the two parties share responsibility for learning, neither really controls learning. For those transitioning from formal to informal learning, that has profound implications:

▶ Objectives often do not exist and, when they do, might be quite broad and not expressed in observable and measurable terms.

▶ Even with these more loosely defined objectives, the lessons actually learned may or may not relate to them.

▶ Learners or circumstances often determine when learning is complete; evaluation is optional and often does not formally occur.

▶ When workers do share what they have learned, the specific lessons each individual takes from the experience are unique because each worker integrates those lessons in ways that relate to their own circumstances, previous knowledge, and current needs.

This personalization of informal learning is particularly powerful, and individualized learning experiences play as significant a role in informal learning as ones shared with groups. The next chapter explores individual opportunities for informal learning.

 Getting It Done

Much informal learning supports the social approach to learning described in this chapter. Some definitions of learning describe it as a "change in behavior," in which learners succeed in their efforts when they adopt behaviors defined in the learning objectives. This definition is rooted in a behaviorist (and, to some extent, cognitivist) view of learning.

But learning often happens as a result of interactions with other people and cultures, which results in the construction of an individual basis of knowledge that is as rooted in culture and context as it is in behaviors. This constructivist approach to learning, as educators call it, underlies much informal learning. Under such views, learning is more than a change in behavior; it is also a change in knowledge, attitudes, perspectives, and, perhaps, beliefs—and the results are not always predictable.

Use Table 5–1 to determine which types of group activities might meet particular informal learning needs of workers in your organization at each phase during the life cycles of their jobs.

Table 5–1. Group Activities That Promote Informal Learning at Different Phases in the Life Cycle of a Job

Orient workers to the technical aspects of a job	Onboard workers to the culture and values of the group	Expand the scope of assignments a worker can handle	Build workers' proficiency	Help workers address undocumented challenges	Update workers' skills and knowledge	Help workers choose career goals	Prepare workers for their next jobs	Address ongoing initiatives
Coaching Formal courses On-the-job training (OJT)	Communities Meetings Networks Peer learning Seminars, symposia, conferences, and webinars	Coaching Communities Formal courses Lunch and learns On-the-job training (OJT) Peer learning.	Coaching Communities Formal courses Lunch and learns Networks On-the-job training (OJT) Peer learning Seminars, symposia, conferences, and webinars	Coaching Communities Lunch and learns Meetings Networks Peer learning Seminars, symposia, conferences, and webinars	Communities Formal courses Lunch and learns Meetings Networks On-the-job training (OJT) Peer learning Seminars, symposia, conferences, and webinars	Coaching Communities Networks Peer learning	Coaching Formal courses Networks On-the-job training (OJT) Peer learning	Formal courses Lunch and learns Meetings Networks On-the-job training (OJT) Peer learning Seminars, symposia, conferences, and webinars

Worksheet 5–1. Supporting Informal Learning Through Group Activities in Your Organization

How might you support informal learning through group activities in your organization? Try these exercises to find out.

1. Billy, who works as a business analyst for a major defense contractor, has responsibility for upgrading content management systems in his organization. He recently saw a conference in Las Vegas that looks like it should provide him with the background he needs to advise his company on future work with these systems, and he asks his manager for work time to travel to the conference, as well as financial support. Because the manager believes that people who attend conferences in Las Vegas spend all of their time in the casinos, the initial reaction is a resounding "No."

   What could the manager do to ensure that Billy has a meaningful conference experience?

   _____

   _____

   _____

   _____

   _____

   Debriefing of exercise 1: If the manager says yes, Billy might not go to the casinos. He might go to the shows and for a tour of Hoover Dam. (Just kidding.)

   The manager can act in these ways as a facilitator to help Billy get the most out of the conference:

   • The manager might ask Billy to provide a list of goals for the conference and then ask which sessions might help Billy meet those goals.

   • Because implementing content management systems poses numerous challenges—from integrating the software into an internal network to adapting work processes so people distribute material through the system rather than through email—networking plays a significant role in the conference. Billy might identify, in advance, networking opportunities that exist.

   • After the conference, the manager might ask Billy either to write a report explaining how he will apply what he has learned at the conference or to deliver a presentation to the rest of the staff with insights gained from the conference—or both.

2. Mozart Publishers (a fictional company) wanted to develop an application for iPads and Android devices through which people could access their magazines online. Mozart publishes 10 magazines but has decided to pilot the effort with just two of them. Anna, the director in charge of the project, recognized that much learning would occur during this project: new technology, new means of delivering content, new ways of writing and presenting material, new means of charging readers and advertisers, and new means of promoting the magazine. Anna did not want any aspect of this learning to go to waste.

So what could she do to capture the learning?

_____

_____

_____

_____

_____

Debriefing of exercise 2: At the least, Anna could create a repository with all project-related materials, such as project proposals, projections, and plans—and revisions to all of them, as well as status reports and other correspondence, and source files for each piece and version of the project.

At the most, Anna might conduct debriefings following key milestones. The debriefings should strive for a balanced view—identifying both what worked and what could be improved (and how)—and should cover each aspect of the project: technical, editorial, financial, marketing, and results. Someone should record the key points in the conversations and include them with the project files.

After the project is complete, Anna might conduct a project postmortem, which would explore the project in its entirety. Like the debriefings at each milestone, the project postmortem should strive for a balanced view—identifying both what worked and what could be improved (and how)—and should cover each aspect of the project: technical, editorial, financial, marketing, and results. In addition, the project postmortem might contain specific recommendations for future projects regarding the process, procedures, technology, content, and business model.

Individual Activities That Promote Informal Learning

What's Inside This Chapter

In this chapter, you'll learn

▶ the personal nature of informal learning
▶ ways that people learn informally through individual experiences and independent activities.

Do you remember Karin, the systems engineer for the software company who helps customers customize their software and troubleshoot problems they cannot solve on their own? She prides herself on her ability to solve really tough problems, which she calls "stump the expert" problems. Documentation rarely addresses the types of problems Karin addresses, so she relies on her experience to solve them. For example, Karin needed to customize a report for a client in the healthcare industry. The report was similar to one she had produced for a client in the financial services industry, so

Karin turned to her notes to see how she had prepared the report and adapted it for the healthcare client. After preparing a draft of the report, she was not sure whether the resulting report met the customer's needs, so she verified hers against a sample the customer had provided.

In this example, Karin learned on the job. She has prior experience, and better records of that experience so she did not need to rely on memory to take advantage of it. She also learned through trial and error and, after succeeding in that, reviewed documentation to figure out how to fulfill an additional customer request. Karin conducted all of this learning independently.

This chapter explores how informal learning occurs through these and similar individual activities. It complements the last chapter, which explored informal learning through group activities. After a brief discussion about the personal nature of learning, this chapter presents two sets of individual activities that promote informal learning—experiential activities and independent learning opportunities.

The Personal Nature of Informal Learning

Although most employers strive for consistency in performance among workers, consistent performance does not mean identical performance. Even though two workers might have had the same training and can perform the same job equally well, they will not perform that job identically because no two workers bring the same body of knowledge and experience to their positions.

Although workers may gain some of the knowledge and experience needed before starting a particular job, they learn much of what they need to know through a combination of experiences that occur on the job and through individual learning. For example, two sales representatives in the same store work in different departments and with different products. Their experiences on the job cause a divergence in these workers' knowledge and skills, even though they received the same basic sales training, because they applied that training differently.

Furthermore, past knowledge and experience reinforces some of this on-the-job learning and contradicts other on-the-job learning. This, in turn, affects the extent to which workers can integrate the lessons, much less benefit from them.

Much learning results from individual experiences and independent activities. Indeed, when they occur, some of these learning opportunities might appear more like entertainment than learning. Such experiences are called *edutainment,* the combination of learning through entertainment. Others feel like marketing but have an instructional message. Such experiences are called *edumarketing*.

This chapter describes 12 specific interventions through which workers learn informally and individually. Like the interventions described in chapter 5, this list is intended to be representative of some of the most common interventions; it is not comprehensive. Similarly as in chapter 5, the descriptions in this chapter explore factors critical to the success of these interventions and ways that training and development professionals can leverage them to support informal learning.

Basic Rule

One of the most powerful ways workers learn informally is through their individual experiences and independent explorations. The lessons learned range from tips that enhance performance on the job to insights gained through failure.

Learning Through Individual Experiences

Experience is a powerful source of knowledge, even if training and development professionals have few tools to quantify it. Consider, for example, the challenge of "selling" an idea to an executive who has strong opinions. A worker who has little or no experience with that executive might approach the task with dread, wondering what button he or she can push to convince the executive that the idea has value. In contrast, the worker who has presented proposals to the executive in the past knows the preferences of the executive and structures the presentation to set off the positive buttons and avoid the negative ones.

So the first set of interventions for informal learning on an individual basis promote learning through experience. Some of the experiences are authentic—they promote learning while workers engage in actual work activities—but others are simulated—they promote learning through re-creations of actual experiences.

Think About This

Because they combine technical and emotional content, experiences lead to powerful learning. Workers observe and practice technical skills through experience. Experience provides the joy of success as well as the frustrations and insights arising from failure. Although training and development professionals cannot design the actual experiences through which workers learn, they can identify such experiences, promote participation in them, and help make explicit some of the insights gained.

Developmental Assignments

Developmental assignments, also known as *stretch assignments*, are projects that help workers build a particular set of skills and prepare them for expanded responsibilities. Some developmental assignments are primary responsibilities. For example, to provide new hires who have high potential with an opportunity to see the breadth of its operations, a bank might rotate workers through a series of six-month assignments over a two-year period. In other instances, the developmental assignment is a secondary responsibility. For example, a manager might try to help a worker build financial acumen by asking that person to track the departmental budget.

Professional internships are also developmental assignments; they are usually brief, full-time assignments that expose workers to different jobs. Workers conduct these internships during the course of their employment. For example, a first-line manager in research and development might work as an intern in the office of the vice president in preparation for a promotion to a middle management position. Professional internships contrast with academic ones. Academic internships are also developmental assignments but occur in the context of a degree program. Professional internships also contrast with other developmental assignments as those other assignments are ongoing, such as adding responsibilities for overseeing the organization's bylaws to the responsibilities of a senior community planner.

According to Cynthia McCauley, the author of *Developmental Assignments: Creating Learning Experiences Without Changing Jobs*, asking workers to accept a challenge is a key to successful developmental assignments. What challenges individual workers, however, differs among people. Some of the many ways to challenge workers include:

▶ expanding the scope of technical responsibilities, such as from a single operation to an entire process

▶ expanding the scope of influence, such as from one department to a group of departments

▶ expanding the scope of managerial responsibilities of a possible management candidate, such as by assigning him or her stewardship of the departmental budget

▶ moving a worker from a well-defined, established project to a new initiative for which neither the product nor the process are fully defined, much less tested.

Although some organizational cultures value the "sink-or-swim" approach to developmental assignments, an approach that is likely to produce more consistent success is assigning workers to developmental assignments for which they are qualified and reasonably prepared but, until now, have not had the opportunity to take on.

Most significantly, because developmental assignments are intended as learning experiences, workers need coaching and feedback on their performance to reflect on the lessons learned. This should occur throughout the assignment, especially at key milestones. Given the nature of many developmental assignments, unless someone is specifically encouraged to offer feedback and reflection, they might not occur.

Training and development professionals can support developmental assignments by doing the following:

▶ Help managers identify appropriate assignments and determine worker readiness.

▶ Help workers realize that they have a responsibility to learn.

▶ Help all parties recognize that some of the learning might result from failure—and teaching them to accept that.

Training and development professionals can also provide resources to help managers and workers reflect on what was learned through this assignment and how workers might apply the lessons. Figure 6–1 suggests how developmental assignments contribute to informal learning.

Figure 6–1. How Developmental Assignments Contribute to Informal Learning

Informal Formal	Informal Formal	Informal Formal	Informal Formal	Informal Formal
Process	**Location**	**Purpose**	**Content**	**Consciousness**
The learning goals of most developmental assignments suggest some externally driven learning process, but workers control most of that process.	Developmental assignments occur in the workplace, not the classroom.	Developmental assignments have an expressed learning agenda, but they also have agendas that extend beyond training.	Although the assignment is intended to develop specific skills and knowledge, workers also develop broader conceptual knowledge about the assignment and its implications.	Because managers often start these assignments by noting that they are learning experiences, workers are somewhat conscious that learning should occur, but they often overlook that fact under the pressure of the actual assignment.

Gaming Simulations

Gaming simulations are learning experiences that replicate the central characteristics of complex situations (that's the simulation part) and that let users experience the consequences of decisions made in those situations (that's the gaming part). Although gaming simulations are usually designed and developed for formal learning, providing workers with ongoing access to the gaming simulations lets them practice how they might handle situations similar to ones they encounter on the job and continue to develop their skills.

Examples of gaming simulations include:

▶ combat, aircraft, and nuclear simulators, which re-create challenging situations, such as disasters, and let workers prepare for situations that have life-or-death consequences in "safe" environments

▶ experiencing-the-other simulations, which sensitize workers to the thoughts and feelings of others, such as a simulation of life as an 85-year-old resident of a nursing home

▶ medical simulators, which often take the form of lifelike dolls with complex programming that lets the doll exhibit a number of medical symptoms and respond to simulated treatments

▶ sales simulations, which are semi-scripted conversations that let workers practice interactions with customers

▶ language learning programs, which provide similar capabilities to sales simulations and let workers develop skills in another language.

Although gaming simulations are often developed for formal learning and with formal learning objectives in mind, participating in gaming simulations often leads learners to deeply personal lessons that go well beyond those anticipated by the designers. Figure 6–2 suggests how gaming simulations contribute to informal learning.

Figure 6–2. How Gaming Simulations Contribute to Informal Learning

Process	Location	Purpose	Content	Consciousness
Informal — Formal	Informal — Formal	Informal — Formal	Informal — Formal	Informal — Formal
Despite the organization formally designing gaming simulations and choosing the types of situations they address, workers choose which scenarios they practice and, as a result, control part of the learning process.	Some simulations may only be used in places intended for learning, such as some aircraft, combat, and medical simulations. Others are used online but are part of a more formal learning program (even if workers are not interacting with the structured parts).	Most gaming simulations are designed with learning in mind, although some are also intended for practice outside the learning environment.	Although gaming simulations are intended to help workers apply technical content, that they immerse workers in the application of processes and procedures helps the workers develop conceptual knowledge.	On one level, workers are conscious of the factual learning they experience through gaming simulations. But they might not be conscious of some of the deeper insights developed through these experiences.

Training and development professionals can support gaming simulations for informal learning in a number of different ways. When choosing gaming simulations for formal courses, consider the possibilities for using them in informal learning and address these possibilities in the design and development effort. In addition, make workers aware that they can use the simulations for practice outside of training, arrange for any necessary support, and provide resources that help workers debrief the simulation activity on their own.

On-the-Job Training (OJT)

On-the-job training refers to a structured program that workers follow to develop a specific set of skills and knowledge needed to perform one or more aspects of their work assignments. On-the-job training usually involves a formal presentation of content—sometimes delivered orally to or read by the worker—then a demonstration of skills and the opportunity to receive feedback from a more experienced worker.

Employers typically use on-the-job training in situations when fewer people need training than would make a class, or when workers need training immediately and cannot wait for a formally scheduled class. Occasionally, employers use on-the-job training for other purposes, such as expanding the scope of assignments that workers can handle and addressing ongoing initiatives. For example, a major insurance provider used on-the-job training to introduce workers to a new computer system.

On-the-job training exhibits many of the characteristics of formal learning, such as formal objectives and structured learning. But because workers participate in on-the-job training individually and on their own schedules, many consider it to be a form of informal learning. In addition, although workers tend to approach on-the-job training as a form of independent study, successful on-the-job training typically involves an experienced worker or manager who guides and tracks the learning process.

Technology supports on-the-job training in a few key ways. Workers typically view the tutorials and other formally prepared materials online, using a computer, tablet, or mobile device. Online checklists can, at the least, remind workers and those overseeing on-the-job training about tasks to be performed and, at the most, track and report the status of those tasks.

Although the planning of on-the-job training is often less rigorous than the planning for a formal training program, it should, at the least, involve the following:

- ▸ concretely defining the tasks and situations the worker should be able to successfully perform at the end of the on-the-job training effort
- ▸ identifying any background information needed
- ▸ considering how to demonstrate the task to the new worker (recording? live demonstration?)
- ▸ deciding whether the worker should perform the task for the first time in a practice situation or on the job
- ▸ determining how to assess worker's performance and competence
- ▸ determining how long the worker should be closely supervised when performing the task before the worker can perform the task on his or her own
- ▸ considering any cultural, interpersonal, or judgment factors that might affect the extent to which the worker achieves the objectives of the on-the-job training program.

After considering all of this, the person planning the on-the-job training might also consider how much material a new worker can master in the given time. Breaking complex tasks into smaller ones helps workers mentally manage the learning process. Similarly, overwhelming workers with complexity on the first day could prevent a second day from occurring.

Although most departments prepare their own on-the-job training, training and development professionals can support these departments by providing templates and similar resources. These templates might include a schedule of on-the-job training that walks departments through the key issues they should consider when preparing an on-the-job training program. Training and development professionals can also provide advice on how to structure an on-the-job training program, how to chunk (divide) job tasks so workers can quickly master them, how much material departments can expect workers to absorb in an hour or a day of on-the-job training, how to assess learning, and how to provide feedback during the on-the-job training process. Figure 6–3 suggests how on-the-job training contributes to informal learning.

Figure 6–3. How On-the-Job Training Contributes to Informal Learning

Process	Location	Purpose	Content	Consciousness
The organization drives the process of formal on-the-job training. But the relationship between the trained worker and the one providing the training often continues after the formal agenda is complete, with the worker usually driving the agenda at that phase.	Much on-the-job training occurs in the workplace. But some on-the-job training involves reading or taking tutorials, activities that might occur in a place intended for learning.	The primary purpose of most on-the-job training is learning. But the interactions between workers that occur during on-the-job training support cultural and team-building goals, which are often conscious goals of this type of intervention.	The primary content of on-the-job training is technical. But through the interaction of workers during the process, abstract concepts are also experienced and perhaps discussed.	Workers are typically conscious of the learning, especially about technical and job-related issues. The one-on-one interaction typical of most on-the-job training, however, often introduces a cultural dimension to the effort, whose lessons workers often learn unconsciously.

Performance Support

Performance support refers to a combination of job aids, guides, reference materials, information in a knowledge base (such as customer and employee records, or a history of calls to the help line), software applications, and other assistance available to workers to help them succeed on the job. Most performance support systems are provided online, resulting in their more common name: *electronic* performance support systems. Software developers are increasingly integrating performance support into applications—especially specialized applications for specific industries or jobs. The commercial software Quicken, for example, is a performance support system for balancing a checkbook and managing personal finances. Travel websites like Travelocity and Expedia are performance support systems for booking travel.

Although the idea of supporting performance in the workplace predates the wide availability of intelligent technology, the emergence of these technologies has spurred practical applications of the concept because they support performance at levels not feasible in earlier times. Wizards guide workers through otherwise complex processes, such as installing software, formatting complex reports, and performing complex calculations—like the load factors on planes. Automatic operations provide reminders, such as the automatic reminders that airlines send ticketed passengers to check in for their flights. Monitoring capabilities of software track worker performance and provide feedback on it so workers can improve performance—as with the auto-correct features in word processing. Intelligent forms automatically fill in information that is already known to the system (such as the information about the worker and the department) so workers only need to complete the new parts—avoiding data entry errors.

Performance support systems are often complex software applications or sophisticated marketing-like campaigns. When Gloria Gery published her landmark 1991 book that introduced them, she envisioned that the ideal performance support system would be seamlessly integrated into the work environment. Twenty years later, many software applications do integrate user support, such as many of the apps for smartphones and tablets.

Gery notes, however, that the key to effective performance support systems is not the technology; it is "in understanding actual job requirements and structuring the information and access methods" so that workers cannot tell where the system ends and the support begins.

Training and development professionals can promote performance support through active participation in efforts to design such resources into software and work environments. Participation includes helping identify the requirements, determining the type of support needed by workers and when they might need it, developing components of the system that meet those needs, introducing the system to workers, and maintaining the system—including updating material in the system and adjusting it in response to feedback from users. Figure 6–4 suggests how performance support contributes to informal learning.

Figure 6–4. How Performance Support Contributes to Informal Learning

Process	Location	Purpose	Content	Consciousness
Informal — Formal	Informal — Formal	Informal — Formal	Informal — Formal	Informal — Formal
The organization designs and develops the system. But effective design processes encourage the organization to actively include workers in the design of systems intended to support them.	Performance support occurs within the context of the job, rather than a place specifically intended for learning.	Performance support focuses on successful completion of a task, rather than instruction on how to perform it.	The majority of content in performance support systems is technical, although some of the more flexible aspects of performance support address more abstract topics.	Because performance support emphasizes doing rather than learning, when workers do learn, they often do so unconsciously.

Trial and Error

As workers learn collectively through work assignments and projects, so can they learn individually through trial and error on the job. Trial and error is one part (admittedly extreme) of the process of practicing skills and developing fluency with them. Workers employ trial and error in situations like these:

▶ When attempting to perform processes that are not documented or for which they are not aware of the documentation; for example, a worker who does not know how to change a customer record might attempt to do so by following the on-screen prompts to see whether he or she can figure it out.

▶ When attempting to improve or expand upon existing processes by trying variations of them; for example, a manager might try to shorten the process for hiring a new worker by seeking two approvals simultaneously rather than asking for one first and then getting the other.

▶ When developing drafts of materials and receiving feedback on them; for example, a new project manager might develop a budget and schedule for a project and then request feedback on it. The resulting comments would help the manager assess the accuracy of the estimates, so he or she can improve the next set of estimates.

▶ When designing a new product or service; for example, product designers and marketers took nearly a decade to find the winning formula and name for the Post-it note. The inventor developed the adhesive without an intended use. A co-worker found an intended use several years later, but the initial product name and sales disappointed. But 3M—the company that makes Post-it notes—valued trial and error and learned from its lessons. The learning experience eventually resulted in a popular product that most people use today (Lemelson-MIT, n.d.; Wikipedia, n.d.).

Two factors affect the extent to which workers learn from trial and error. First, workers need feedback on their performance. If they have no idea whether their trial resulted in success, partial success, or failure, they cannot hope to re-create the performance should a similar situation arise in the future. Second, workers need to feel comfortable failing. They should not feel that their jobs are threatened by an occasional honest failure. The lesson learned through that failure could have a long-term benefit to the organization. Many organizational cultures discourage failure—some consciously, others unconsciously. This discourages workers from seeking advice and corrective feedback from co-workers. Feeling comfortable telling co-workers about a failure could help workers resolve a potentially serious situation and avoid failures in the future.

Training and development professionals can support learning from trial and error by sensitizing management to the value of learning from failure and the dangers of punishing workers for unintentional failures. Figure 6–5 suggests how trial and error contributes to informal learning.

Figure 6–5. How Trial and Error Contributes to Informal Learning

Process	Location	Purpose	Content	Consciousness
Trial and error usually happens within the context of a job task; workers structure the learning component.	Nearly all trial and error occurs within the context of the job, not in a classroom or place for intentional learning.	Most trials occur just to see whether something works.	Lessons address the technical aspects of the job as well as more abstract content, such as the intricacies of interpersonal interactions.	Workers are conscious of some of the lessons learned through trial and error.

Independent Learning Opportunities

The second set of interventions for independent informal learning involves study, some of it actively sought by the worker but some of it passive—in which content is brought to the worker.

The following sections explore several types of independent activities that contribute to informal learning and suggest when and how you might use them in the life cycle of a job.

Think About This

Although some informal learning happens unconsciously, workers actively initiate and engage in much of it. Training and development professionals can support workers in their efforts to learn independently by making sure that they can easily find content of interest and, when they do, that they can easily comprehend it.

Advertising

Within the context of informal learning, advertising refers to short promotional messages that serve these purposes:

- ▶ Build awareness about an issue; for example, the human resources departments of many organizations promote one or more employee benefits at various times throughout the year, such as employee assistance, adoption assistance, and tuition reimbursement programs. Workers might not need these programs when they encounter the message, but the human resources staff hopes to increase the likelihood that employees will recall the availability of these programs when the need arises.
- ▶ To call for immediate action; for example, each autumn, many U.S. companies advertise the healthcare options available so that workers will choose the program and coverage that best meets their needs before the enrollment deadline.

Although advertisements play a significant role in informal learning, their primary role is building awareness of, and interest and participation in, informal learning opportunities. They are not intended as a vehicle of instruction.

Typical advertisements are short: a single poster, a pictorial email message, a brief letter, or a 30-second to one-minute video or slide show. The primary exception is a catalog, which is, essentially, a compendium of advertisements.

Technology supports the creation and distribution of advertising. Most organizations use the home pages of their corporate and departmental intranet sites, email, and social networking to distribute advertising to workers. Although much of this promotion has a certain "broadcast" quality to it—that is, it comes from the authorities to the people—these same media often provide workers with the opportunity to share their own messages within their departments and organizations, and social networking tools provide workers with opportunities to comment on the messages.

Training and development professionals can support advertising by identifying issues and topics to address in advertising, making sure that the advertisements are distributed and viewed as widely as possible and, when workers respond to the ads, making sure that the promised services and resources are available. Figure 6–6 suggests how advertisements contribute to informal learning.

Figure 6–6. How Advertisements Contribute to Informal Learning

Process	Location	Purpose	Content	Consciousness
Informal — Formal	Informal — Formal	Informal — Formal	Informal — Formal	Informal — Formal
The "advertiser" controls the learning process, often designing the advertisement to elicit a particular emotional response.	Workers are expected to encounter advertising messages in their work contexts, not in learning contexts.	Learning is a secondary purpose of advertising.	The content of some advertisements is technical, intended for immediate application. The content of other advertisements is abstract, intended for long-term awareness. Both types of advertisements acknowledge "what," but do not explain "how" or "why."	Because advertisements have short, tightly focused messages, learners are often conscious of what they have learned. At the same time, because many advertisements focus on awareness, learners might store the message and recall it much later.

Case Studies

In the context of informal learning, case studies are structured reports about past experiences. A complete case study describes the problem or challenge faced, requirements for a solution, selection and development of a solution, subsequent results with the solution, and lessons learned from the experience. Case studies can come from within the organization or from outside sources. Typically, organizations only like to promote case studies of successful projects, but as consultant and professor Richard Swanson and his co-author John Zuber (1996) noted, case studies of failure often provide some of the most valuable learning material.

In informal learning, workers typically find case studies in trade and professional publications, on websites, and on intranets. Research suggests that workers value case studies because they describe both abstract and technical content within the contexts of projects like the ones on which they work.

Many workers explore case studies on their own, not in the classroom, with limited opportunities (if any) to discuss the cases with colleagues. As a result, the more complete the case, the more information that workers have available to them to explore its applications to their work environment.

This completeness also contributes to the credibility of the case (Vosecky, Siegel, and Wallace, 2008). One characteristic of completeness involves providing readers with sufficient detail about the case so they can follow it. Another characteristic is balance: describing not only what went right, but what went wrong, even if the case documents a success. This balance contributes to the richness of the learning as well as to the credibility of the case.

Another important characteristic of effective cases is explicitly stated implications. The more directly and clearly stated are the implications, the more likely workers can apply the case to their own situations.

Training and development professionals can support the development and dissemination of case studies. They can provide templates to prepare cases and then encourage workers in the organization to document them. Training and development professionals can also encourage workers and their managers to document unsuccessful cases, so other workers can learn from their failures. Additionally, training and development professionals can support the use of case studies by developing and maintaining a central storage place—or *repository*—for cases to be used by workers. Figure 6–7 suggests how case studies contribute to informal learning.

Figure 6–7. How Case Studies Contribute to Informal Learning

Process	Location	Purpose	Content	Consciousness
Someone prepares the case because they feel it contains insights from which others can learn. But workers determine which cases they read and which lessons they take from the cases.	Workers read case studies within the context of their job or outside of their job, rather than in a location intended for learning.	Authors prepare case studies specifically to illuminate some aspect of work to readers, so that workers learn from the authors' experiences.	Although focused on application, the nature of case study content is somewhat abstract, helping workers develop abstract reasoning processes about work situations.	Workers are somewhat conscious of learning that occurs by reading case studies.

Documentation

Documentation is a general term that refers to the policies, processes, procedures, product descriptions, product plans, reports, and similar materials describing the operations of an organization and the products and services that organization offers. These sources are often a primary tool that workers use to informally learn about their jobs.

At its best, documentation provides workers with a clear, concise overview of the technical content they need to perform their jobs. At its worst, documentation takes the form of a stack of minimally organized materials that greets new workers their first day on the job. "Read this," someone usually tells the new worker. "It tells you everything you need to know."

Traditionally, organizations have printed documentation, but it is now increasingly available online, usually managed through content management systems. As organizations have moved their documentation online, they have added social media capabilities to it. Two increasingly popular forms of documentation let members of the community that use the documents contribute to, or completely write, the documents:

▸ SME-authored documentation refers to documentation written partially or entirely by subject matter experts (SMEs). This documentation usually has the authority of technical expertise, though it often lacks the practicality of everyday use.
▸ User-generated documentation refers to documentation written partially or entirely by the people who use the content daily. This documentation usually has the authority of actual field use.

Although many books and websites describe the characteristics of effective documentation and offer tips and techniques for writing specific types of documents, these key characteristics boil down to completeness, usability, and accuracy (including whether the documentation is up-to-date).

People other than training and development professionals create much of the documentation on which workers rely. However, training and development professionals can still support the development of documentation by providing templates to guide authors through the process of preparing documents and ensuring that the documents appear consistent to users. Training and development professionals can also recommend documents that might benefit particular groups of workers at various phases in the life spans of their jobs. Training and development professionals can also monitor documents and inform the groups that published them when the documents are either out-of-date or inconsistent with other documents used in the organization. Figure 6–8 suggests how documentation contributes to informal learning.

Figure 6–8. How Documentation Contributes to Informal Learning

Process	Location	Purpose	Content	Consciousness
Informal — Formal	Informal — Formal	Informal — Formal	Informal — Formal	Informal — Formal
Except for user-generated documents, the organization controls the process for creating documentation.	Workers typically use documentation in their work areas rather than in a place specifically intended for learning.	Documentation is provided for a variety of reasons, such as ensuring consistency among workers and learning.	Documentation typically addresses technical aspects of a job and guides workers in performing tasks.	In some instances, workers are conscious they are learning. In other cases, they believe they are merely checking a fact they'll forget later. But they might actually retain the material.

Guided Tours

Guided tours are brief (30 seconds to five minutes) online presentations that explain what a topic is and why it's important; guided tours do not explain how to perform a task. Guided tours provide more content than advertisements, which raise awareness or represent a call to action, but less than tutorials and documentation, which describe concepts and skills in depth.

Although all guided tours are online, they come in a variety of forms, such as Flash movies, self-running PowerPoint presentations, and static—though visually enticing—webpages. In a well-coordinated campaign, a guided tour would follow an advertisement and answer the next question, "What is this issue and, at a high level, how would I apply it?" That, in turn, should entice viewers to formally learn about the topic. Examples of guided tours include an overview of benefits available to workers, or an overview of a new learning management system.

Training and development professionals can support guided tours by developing them when appropriate and advising others in the organization to develop them to accompany other materials they prepare. Training and development professionals might also prepare templates to help others create guided tours and promote their availability to workers and their managers. Figure 6–9 suggests how guided tours contribute to informal learning.

Figure 6–9. How Guided Tours Contribute to Informal Learning

Process	Location	Purpose	Content	Consciousness
The organization controls the process for creating and distributing guided tours (except when workers distribute the links themselves).	Workers view guided tours in places other than those intended for formal learning.	Guided tours are primarily developed with an instructional agenda, though they can be purely informational.	Guided tours typically provide conceptual overviews of technical content.	Although most workers are aware that they are learning, some might not intend to retain or apply the information.

(Each column shows a gauge ranging from "Informal" to "Formal.")

Independent Research and Study

Independent research and study refers to efforts by workers to investigate topics and develop expertise in them. Sometimes workers initiate the project, and sometimes the employer does.

The end result of independent research and study varies, depending on who has initiated the effort and the intended use of what has been learned. At its most informal, independent research and study results in an expanded base of knowledge for the worker. At its most formal, independent research and study can result in a formal report and, perhaps, recommendations for action, such as adoption of new policies, processes, or technologies, or proposals for new products or services.

Technology plays a crucial role in supporting independent study and research. Consider, for example, a worker who participates in an online community about social media. Someone mentions an unfamiliar term in the conversation. Curious, the worker performs a Google search to find more information and finds an entry in Wikipedia. Wikipedia provides a brief definition and concludes with several citations. The worker clicks on a link to an article in *BusinessWeek* magazine online and learns more. While there, the worker notices the list of most popular articles and sees one of interest—which starts a new independent study effort about a different topic.

Several factors affect the quality of independent study and research. The most fundamental are strong search and retrieval skills. Consider the problem faced by help line technicians in the case study reported by Downing (2006), which was first mentioned in chapter 2. In that study, Downing found that when customers called with problems the technicians did not understand, the technicians would use Google or a similar search engine to find relevant documents in the company knowledge base (while the customer waited on the phone, of course). Downing notes that

> if the keyword that technicians typed into the tool did not adequately match the index or metadata housed within the tool, the tool rarely provided Client Logic technicians with a correct solution.
>
> ▶ The broader the keyword, the more documents the tool returned.
> ▶ Even "appropriate" keyword queries produced too many hits on the results page to be useful to technicians.
> ▶ Team members noticed that using the existing tool actually *increased* technicians' average handle time. This result led some technicians to become frustrated and choose a solution—one solution among the numerous options listed from the unsuccessful query—to try to solve the customer's issue (p. 205).

Often, that solution was not correct, resulting in a callback, reduced customer satisfaction, and all sorts of other problems. The organization addressed this problem by requiring that workers go through a prescribed series of questions at the beginning of the call, which would lead them to information that would solve about 80 percent of the issues that usually prompted the calls.

Other factors besides poor search and retrieval skills affect the quality of independent study. One is information that has been improperly labeled or is written poorly. Another is lack of access to content of interest. Although much information is available for free on the Internet, some of the most valuable reports, research, and professional literature is not. Commercial databases usually provide access to these articles. So do university libraries. But workers who lack access to these resources lack access to the valuable information they provide. So although independent study supports a laudable goal of independently developing knowledge, skills, and attitudes, the process on its own can be inefficient and unproductive.

In instances where the types of issues workers need to study are known, training and development professionals can follow the lead of Client Logic and require that workers go through a prescribed search process to find information of interest—which also helps those who create the information to properly index it.

For sustained independent study about a particular topic, workers might benefit from a more formal study plan. Like the learning contracts proposed by the advocates of self-directed learning, these study plans help workers formalize their goals, consult with others about appropriate resources to study, determine what they hope to learn from each, and, after using a resource, assess what they learned and how it added to their knowledge and skills. Figure 6–10 provides a template for an independent study plan.

Figure 6–10. Template for an Independent Study Plan

Topic You Plan to Study

_____

_____

_____

Why You Are Studying This Topic

_____

_____

_____

What You Hope to Learn

_____

_____

_____

How You Hope to Use the Skills and Knowledge

_____

_____

_____

(continued)

Figure 6–10. Template for an Independent Study Plan (continued)

Whom You Plan to Consult for Advice and Insights

1. _____

2. _____

3. _____

Sources You Plan to Consult

Source	Why You Plan to Use It	What You Learned From It
_____	_____	_____
_____	_____	_____
_____	_____	_____
_____	_____	_____

How You Plan to Demonstrate What You Have Learned (So You Can Assess the Extent to Which You Have Learned It)

_____

_____

_____

Training and development professionals can support informal research and study by

▶ promoting the information search, retrieval, and assessment skills that help workers become more productive and effective in research efforts

▶ working with internal groups so that the content they publish is indexed for easy retrieval, and the material is clear and consistent so workers can comprehend it on the first read-through

▶ encouraging organizations to subscribe to information sources that contain relevant content for their work, and then encouraging workers to use these sources.

Figure 6–11 suggests how independent study and research contribute to informal learning.

Figure 6–11. How Independent Study and Research Contribute to Informal Learning

Process	Location	Purpose	Content	Consciousness
Informal — Formal	Informal — Formal	Informal — Formal	Informal — Formal	Informal — Formal
Learners completely drive this process, from choosing the topic to study to assessing what they learned. They might seek advice along the way, but at their own initiative.	Learning can happen anywhere, but when workers are intentionally studying, they often choose places that are conducive to learning, such as a library.	Workers conduct independent research and study to learn, but also often to complete a job task they are in the middle of.	Although some workers approach independent study and research to learn technical content, most enter it with a broader agenda that includes conceptual knowledge.	Sometimes workers are conscious of the learning; in other instances, they might think they are merely conducting a search for information that they may or may not retain.

Tips and Tricks

Tips and tricks refer to a class of articles and books that describe skills and knowledge that are not required in a job, but can increase the productivity of the reader. Tips-and-tricks articles typically appear in popular professional publications including magazines, webzines, and websites, or as popular series of books, such as the *Dummies* books, which were originally intended for computer users but were eventually extended to include many other subject areas such as eldercare and knitting. (The *Basics* series from ASTD is an example of tips and tricks.)

Tips-and-tricks articles and books typically explain how to do something or how something affects readers. They cover topics such as

▶ technology
▶ use of particular products or classes of products
▶ professional skills
▶ interpersonal skills.

Technology supports tips and tricks in several ways:

- ▶ Publishers increasingly distribute the tips and tricks online, through either websites (typically used for articles) or e-books (used for books and magazines).
- ▶ Readers use social media, especially Twitter, to share articles whose tips and tricks they found helpful.
- ▶ Some people share their own tips—individually through blogs and collectively through wikis.

Successful tips and tricks have the following characteristics, which all boil down to usefulness:

- ▶ relevance (tips that workers can apply in their jobs)
- ▶ timeliness (tips that workers can use now)
- ▶ clarity (tips that are written in a language and style that workers can quickly comprehend on the first read-through, such as "five tips for . . . " or "seven steps to . . . ")
- ▶ findability (encountering tips in places where workers are likely to look for them).

By promoting the sharing of tips and tricks, training and development professionals can raise awareness of these resources in their organizations and guide others to share their own tips and tricks. Training and development professionals can also encourage groups in their organizations to provide spots for tips-and-tricks articles on their intranet sites as well as on social media sites such as Twitter and company blogs, or through links in email messages. Figure 6–12 suggests how tips and tricks contribute to informal learning.

Figure 6–12. How Tips and Tricks Contribute to Informal Learning

Process	Location	Purpose	Content	Consciousness
Informal — Formal	Informal — Formal	Informal — Formal	Informal — Formal	Informal — Formal
Tips and tricks are typically provided by one group of workers for another.	Workers typically read tips and tricks in locations other than those intended for learning.	Some tips and tricks are informational, which workers read and then forget; others are instructional, which workers retain.	Most of the content of tips and tricks tends to be technical or procedural, but some articles address more abstract content.	Although some workers approach tips and tricks as a quick learning opportunity, others approach them as information to be used immediately and then forgotten. In such instances, longer term learning is unconscious.

Tutorials

In the context of informal learning, tutorials are asynchronous online lessons that workers take at their own convenience because they believe the tutorials will help them develop knowledge or skills in an area of interest.

These interests may or may not completely match the learning objectives. For example, a worker who would like to learn how to format headings in Excel spreadsheets might take an advanced Excel formatting tutorial that also addresses formatting other parts of the spreadsheet. Workers may take the entire tutorial or only the parts of interest to them.

In the workplace, tutorials used for informal learning come from a variety of sources. There are

- off-the-shelf tutorials
- product and process tutorials from suppliers and customers
- tutorials from professional and trade associations
- tutorials from government agencies and nonprofits
- university courses and tutorials from nonprofit associations, such as those offered by the MIT Open Courseware project or through iTunes University.

The material addressed in these tutorials ranges from factual knowledge intended for recall to complex analysis skills that sensitize workers to situations they might encounter.

Most tutorials used for informal learning were developed for formal purposes. Some characteristics that make them effective in informal learning situations include

- clearly stated objectives and agenda, which help learners determine whether the tutorial addresses topics that are of interest to them and the extent to which it does so
- fast-paths through the content, so workers can take a quick look to determine whether they feel comfortable performing the skill and, if they do, easily leave the tutorial having gained the skills and knowledge they sought
- no prerequisites, so workers who lack time for the prerequisites can still explore the content
- optional self-assessment tools, which are tests that assess the extent to which workers have acquired the skills and knowledge. (Self-assessments provide results in a consultative way, so workers can determine whether they need to continue learning. The results are not shared with the employer.)

In addition to designing and developing tutorials, training and development professionals can support the use of tutorials for informal learning by making sure that the ones they design—as well as the ones they purchase for their employers—possess the characteristics described earlier. When choosing tutorials designed by others, select those that best support informal learning. Figure 6–13 suggests how tutorials contribute to informal learning.

Figure 6–13. How Tutorials Contribute to Informal Learning

Process	Location	Purpose	Content	Consciousness
Informal — Formal	Informal — Formal	Informal — Formal	Informal — Formal	Informal — Formal
Although the organization controls the process of creating the tutorial itself, the worker controls the process of determining the extent to which the tutorial meets his or her learning needs.	Tutorials can be taken anywhere workers have access to the content. But because most workers start tutorials with the intention of learning, the place is usually suitable for that purpose.	Tutorials are designed for learning.	Most tutorials address technical content, though some address conceptual topics.	Workers are conscious of learning when they take tutorials.

A Note About Formality and Informal Learning

The descriptions of each intervention presented in the past two chapters have suggested how each addresses the "levers" of informal learning. But a quick look at the levers shows that none of the levers on any single intervention all face toward the informal learning side of the gauge. In practical terms, that means that most interventions intended for informal learning in the workplace have a certain formality to them. That's because the focus on informal learning in this book is on job-related learning.

In most jobs, workers establish some, but not all, of the responsibilities and content of their jobs. Employers define some or all of the scope of responsibilities as well as the policies, processes, and procedures under which workers perform their jobs. Even self-employed workers have clients who define the nature of the jobs they perform.

In other words, as noted earlier at the beginning of this chapter, informal learning acknowledges that, for certain aspects of a job, organizations have preferences for the approach that workers take to their work. This is reflected in the formalized aspects of the interventions. But many organizations also recognize the individuality in the ways that workers approach tasks, and informal learning promotes this individuality.

More than merely communicating technical content, however, informal learning helps workers build attitudes toward their work. Some activities help workers build their self-awareness; others help them develop feelings of *self-efficacy*—an educational term that refers to learners' feelings of confidence that they can perform tasks. Although some workers might initiate informal learning at the suggestion or example of others, many initiate the effort on their own, when they are ready to develop their skills, knowledge, and attitudes.

What this means for training and development professionals is that the types of control that our profession emphasizes for formal learning programs are not practical in informal learning, in which workers learn what they choose to learn when they choose to learn it. When learning needs match those identified by the organization, training and development professionals can play an active role in creating the experiences and resources used for informal learning and encouraging workers to take advantage of them.

But much of informal learning focuses on individual lessons, many of which cannot be anticipated or planned. In those instances, the challenge is to help workers become conscious of their learning so that they are aware of how it affects them and, if appropriate, receive recognition for it.

Getting It Done

Training and development professionals help workers achieve their learning goals by suggesting one or a combination of the interventions mentioned in this chapter. Table 6–1 guides you in this task by suggesting specific informal and individual learning interventions that can support common learning needs on the job. In the process of matching workers with interventions, you might need to help the workers clarify their goals to ensure the closest possible match and to provide coaching and other types of guidance to help them reflect on and apply what they have learned.

Table 6–1. Specific Informal and Individual Learning Interventions That Support Common Learning Needs on the Job

Orient workers to the technical aspects of a job	Onboard workers to the culture and values of the group	Expand the scope of assignments a worker can handle	Build workers' proficiency	Help workers address undocumented challenges	Update workers' skills and knowledge	Help workers choose career goals	Prepare workers for their next jobs	Address ongoing initiatives
Documentation	Advertising	Advertising	Advertising	Advertising	Advertising	Advertising	Developmental assignments	Advertising
Guided tours	Case studies	Case studies	Case studies	Case studies	Case studies	Case studies	Documentation	Case studies
	Mentoring	Developmental assignments	Developmental assignments	Documentation	Documentation	Developmental assignments	Gaming simulations	Documentation
		Documentation	Documentation	Gaming simulations	Guided tours	Documentation	Independent research and study	Gaming simulations
		Gaming simulations	Gaming simulations	Guided tours	Mentoring	Gaming simulations	Mentoring	Guided tours
		Guided tours	Guided tours	Independent research and study	Performance support	Guided tours	Tips and tricks	Performance support
		Independent research and study	Independent research and study	Mentoring	Tips and tricks	Independent research and study		Tips and tricks
		Mentoring	Mentoring	Performance support		Mentoring		
		Performance support	Performance support	Tips and tricks		Trial and error		
		Tips and tricks	Tips and tricks	Trial and error				
		Trial and error	Trial and error					

Worksheet 6–1. Exercises

How might you support informal learning through independent activities in your organization? Try these exercises to find out.

1. Colleen is a corporate trainer who has made the initial transition from the face-to-face classroom to the virtual classroom. She participated in a certificate program for experienced classroom trainers, and as a result of the training and practice she received there, the virtual classroom no longer intimidates Colleen. But she has only taught a few classes virtually, and after each, she noted that she still does not feel the sense of comfort in the virtual classroom that she feels in the face-to-face one. She seeks advice on ways to build her comfort and expand her teaching repertoire for the virtual classroom.

    What do you suggest?

    _____

    _____

    _____

    _____

    _____

    Debriefing of exercise 1: Colleen is at the phase of her job where she is seeking to perform more proficiently. A few individual learning efforts might help her achieve this goal:

    - Reading tips and tricks articles for virtual classroom trainers. Some might provide suggestions that Colleen might try.
    - Trial and error. After trying in her virtual classroom the techniques she has learned through tips and tricks articles, Colleen might reflect on which techniques worked, which ones partially worked, and which ones flopped—and why that happened. The reflection process can help her adjust the techniques so they work in her classroom.

    In addition, Colleen might debrief her developmental experiences of teaching online. Crucial to this process is reviewing feedback on course evaluation forms. Students often have insights into what's working and what could be improved, and the feedback could help Colleen prioritize different facets of the next phase of her development as a virtual instructor.

2. Lindsay develops a database that is intended to be used by people who market products and services to businesses. Lindsay admits that she has an aversion to sales reps, which makes her work on the database ironic. In early product tests, these marketing representatives have commented that Lindsay's designs are "clunky." In interviews with people who tested the product, one commented, "Whoever designed this clearly has no idea about what a marketing rep does for a living." Lindsay resisted the comments at first, saying that she was merely following the product specifications. But when her manager commented that "the

specifications merely say what the product needs to do—it's your job to figure out how," Lindsay realized something was amiss. So she asked, "How can I better understand what these marketing representatives do?"

What can you suggest?

_____

_____

_____

_____

_____

Debriefing of exercise 2: The primary issue is that Lindsay has no idea about how marketing representatives conduct their work, and to some extent, she proudly has not cared. The poor response to the product and the direct feedback from her manager have helped Lindsay to start caring. But she still has no concept of the daily routine of the people who use her product, nor of the way that her software can simplify that routine. One of the best ways for Lindsay to develop that sensitivity is by experiencing life as a marketing representative. So she might take a brief internship—a type of developmental assignment—during which she shadows a marketing representative for several days, observes the types of tasks this person performs and how this person works, and considers ways that software might simplify these tasks. Afterward, Lindsay might study again reports about the target market for the product. With her field experience, she might see things in the reports that she has overlooked in the past.

How to Use Technology to Support Informal Learning

What's Inside This Chapter

In this chapter, you'll learn

▶ the difference between learning and information sharing, and the role of technology in supporting both

▶ the six categories of technology and media used with informal learning.

Perhaps you remember Casey, the new assistant manager at a clothing store in the mall, from earlier chapters. She receives training on some of the technical aspects of her job through e-learning, and she uses online "tips of the week" to build her proficiency on the job.

Perhaps you also remember Ricardo, the customer service agent who's looking for his next career opportunity. To start his search, he visits an online career center and takes an online self-assessment to identify positions that might build on his current base of skills and experience.

Consider, too, Curtis, the site supervisor for a construction firm, who misunderstood the human resources policies and procedures in his organization. What's worse, had he taken a moment to check the company intranet (available through his smartphone), he could have checked the policy—and even chatted live with a representative from human resources.

Then consider Marley, the once-unfocused junior account executive with an advertising agency, who has become an expert in business-to-business sales. She did so through a combination of online mentoring, a course on business-to-business marketing that she took online through a marketing communication association, and by following a couple of popular bloggers online.

Last, consider Karin, the systems engineer for a software company, who helps customers customize their software and troubleshoot problems—usually addressing issues that even she has not dealt with before. She participates in an online group of systems engineers in her company, which uses social networking software to communicate with its members. Karin finds not only that the members of the discussion board provide timely responses to her questions, she also finds that she's asking fewer of them because she's learning from the responses that some of her colleagues post. And she has to admit, she sometimes logs on to see where people come from. The two that have impressed her the most in the past month are the systems engineer from Ulanbaatar, Mongolia, and a couple from Chile and Argentina who communicate with one another in Spanish.

Despite the differences in the learning needs of Casey, Ricardo, Curtis, Marley, and Karin, technology plays a significant role in addressing all of them. As noted in chapter 1, the rapid growth of technology has significantly contributed to interest in, and acceptance of, informal learning. But no single technology addresses all learning needs. Some workers use older technologies like e-learning and online documents. Others use newer technologies like smartphones and social networking.

This chapter explores how to use technology and media for informal learning. But first, it pauses to differentiate between two common—and frequently confused—roles of technology in learning.

Two Common—and Frequently Confused—Roles of Technology

One of the unique benefits of the Internet is its capacity to quickly distribute information. For example, imagine that someone in Barcelona heard about a staff change in the offices in New York. So the worker in Barcelona contacts co-workers in the same department—but who work in Los Angeles—for more information. They do not know, so one of them contacts a co-worker whose cubicle is across from the person in New York whose job was affected. The person in New York tells the person in Los Angeles, who in turn tells the person in Barcelona.

The primary role of technology in this example is *information sharing*, not learning. Information sharing involves the exchange of factoids that have interest to people but that do not enhance the skills or knowledge of workers. Information sharing contrasts with *instruction:* exchanges intended to enhance skills and knowledge. Examples of instruction include a description of how to distinguish between counterfeit and real currency, an explanation of the rules that determine which of five claims would be eligible for insurance coverage, and a clarification of a formula for assessing the performance of particular types of aircraft. In most instances, instruction is accompanied by activities and other materials for developing the new skills.

This distinction between instruction and information sharing is essential when discussing technology. Technology has the potential to record, store, and transmit countless factoids. On their own, the factoids are just information: facts and concepts that might have immediate application but have no long-term benefit. In contrast, instruction promotes learning by leading to a change in behavior. Just because technology facilitates both the sharing of information and instruction does not make the two tasks equivalent.

Making this distinction and addressing it increases the likelihood that a particular technology will provide the desired learning benefits.

Basic Rule

When thinking about ways to integrate technology, think about more than sharing information for immediate use—think about ways to build skills, knowledge, and attitudes for the long term.

Technology Used for Informal Learning

Training and development professionals can use a variety of technologies to support informal learning in their organizations. Whether those technologies really support informal learning or merely share information is determined in part by the context of the situation and, in part, by the manner in which training and development professionals promote the materials and the type of support with which they surround these technologies.

This section describes these technologies. To facilitate your understanding of the technologies, it categorizes them as follows:

- ▶ devices used, such as computers, smartphones, and tablets, to access content
- ▶ media used, such as printed material or social media platforms, to deliver content
- ▶ technologies that facilitate learning throughout organizations.

Each section defines its class of technologies, identifies several specific technologies you can use, and explores potential issues or problems associated with those technologies.

Devices Used for Informal Learning

Whether workers want to check in with their online communities of practice, view an instructional video, or read a textbook online, they must perform these tasks on some sort of physical device, such as a computer, an e-book reader, or a smartphone. Several devices support informal learning. See Table 7–1 for a comprehensive list.

Think About This

The many choices of devices used for informal learning, their overlapping capabilities, and the variety of preferences among workers often means that many training and development professionals who support informal learning have to create materials that work on many different types of devices. This, in turn, adds to the workload and its complexity.

Table 7–1. Devices Used for Informal Learning

Category of Devices	Description
Audiovisual equipment	Lets users record and view images and sound, such as video and film recordings, and audiotapes and records. In terms of informal learning, people use audiovisual equipment to create and view instructional videos, inspirational audiobooks, and podcasts.
Printed matter	Books, periodicals, and brochures that contain content for informal learning. Examples include textbooks and professional literature, workbooks for courses, job aids, references, and catalogs of learning opportunities.
E-book readers	Electronic devices that let people read digital versions of printed material. Although specific features vary among devices, e-book readers can read books aloud and let users take notes, adjust type, and bookmark pages (among other capabilities). The software they use can also be used on computers, tablets, and mobile devices. In terms of informal learning, the same types of materials that appear in printed publications usually appear as e-books.
Computers	In terms of informal learning, people use computers to take self-study courses, search for information in references and websites, view overview videos (also called *guided tours*), participate in *webinars* (lectures and courses offered on the Internet), receive ongoing tips and ideas, track their learning, and view articles and other materials.
Tablets	Tablets are flat devices that look like tiny television screens, though they are barely thicker than a piece of cardboard and are easily carried by hand. Tablet computers have many of the same capabilities as computers, but they have limited storage capacity. In terms of informal learning, tablets play similar roles to two other devices: computers and e-book readers. In fact, some tablets have their own e-book reading software.
Mobile devices	Handheld devices such as cell phones, smartphones, MP3 players, portable game players, and personal digital assistants (PDAs). In terms of informal learning, people use mobile devices to play audio and video recordings on the go, as a quick reference, and for ongoing communication with others in their learning communities.

Here are some specific issues to consider when using these devices for informal learning:

- ▶ Affordability, which affects the likelihood that workers can use a particular device. At the time of the publication of this book, prices range from about $100 for some smartphones and e-book readers to several thousand dollars for fully equipped computers.

- ▶ Portability, which refers to how easily users can take the devices from one place to another. Mobile devices, e-book readers, tablets, and printed materials are the most portable; users can read them while riding planes and subways, at the beach, and in bed. The more portable the device, the more flexible the opportunities for learning.

- ▶ Versatility, which refers to the range of tasks people can perform with the device. For example, some e-book readers only let workers read text and an occasional figure, while tablets and desktop computers not only let workers read, but also create documents, watch videos, listen to recordings, communicate, and browse the web. In informal learning, single-purpose devices help focus learners. Versatile devices admittedly offer distractions, but they let workers perform a wide variety of tasks without switching to another device.

- ▶ Interoperability, which refers to the ability of the device to record and display materials in a variety of formats. The more interoperable the device, the fewer devices an individual needs. For example, some e-book readers can only read e-books in certain formats. If workers want to read books in a different format, they need a different device. Similarly, although some tablets can play audiovisual materials, they do not let users record presentations and limit participation in webinars and similar types of live online events.

- ▶ "Coolness," which refers to the desirability of the device. Some devices are admittedly more desirable than others. For example, the iPad was not only the first tablet computer, but as of the publication of this book, it continues to be the most desirable.

Media Used to Deliver Content to Workers

Media used to deliver content to workers include

- classic (noncomputerized) media, such as printed materials, classrooms and meeting rooms, and older recordings
- *core* technologies, also known as web 1.0 technologies, which promote recording and wide distribution of information
- *social media,* also known as web 2.0 technologies, which encourage interaction among individuals (perhaps learners or learners and instructors).

Classic Media Used in Informal Learning

Learners engaged in informal learning long before the arrival of computers and mobile devices, and a variety of media facilitated that learning. Although the use of these media in their traditional formats is declining, the materials continue to exist, and people continue to use them. See Table 7–2 for a list of classic media that facilitate informal learning.

Table 7–2. Classic Media Used With Informal Learning

Category of Classic Media	Description
Printed matter	Described in Table 7–1.
Live events, such as lectures, exhibitions, meetings, and conferences	People from several locations gather in a single place. Events typically occur in meeting rooms, auditoriums, classrooms, and similar spaces built for the purpose of interacting.
Audio recordings	Recorded messages with only a sound track. The messages were originally delivered on records, then on audiotape (including the cassette and 8-track formats), and more recently on compact discs (CDs) and Digital Versatile Discs (DVDs). Listening to audio recordings requires that people have specialized playback equipment, like record, tape, CD, and DVD players.

(continued)

Table 7–2. Classic Media Used With Informal Learning (continued)

Videos	Recorded messages that contain both visual and audio tracks. The messages are delivered on videotapes. The most popular consumer format was VHS, but other formats existed, especially among professional video editors, producers, and directors, as the other formats provided higher quality recordings. Watching video recordings required that people have specialized playback equipment, including a monitor or television screen on which to view the video, and a video cassette recorder that could play recorded videos and record new videos from television.
	Alternatives to video recordings include films, filmstrips, and slide/sound presentations. Films work much like videos, except that they record sound and images on a different type of material and, therefore, require different playback equipment (film projectors and screens) and different recording equipment (film cameras).
	Filmstrips and slide/sound presentations showed still pictures during a narrated presentation. Filmstrips played on special projectors, and slide/sound presentations played on slide machines with tape recorders. Special, barely audible sounds in the presentations would automatically cause the equipment to advance to the next image in the presentation.

Think About This

Although digital media have replaced many of these classic media, materials still exist in these media and interest in them remains. Consider the revival of vinyl records in the music industry and the persistance of live events.

The primary issue to consider when using any predigital medium is the availability of devices to play or display the content. For example, VHS videotapes might contain some valuable lessons, but finding a VHS video player on which to play them poses a challenge. The same problem exists with audiotapes. The one holdout to change is the live event, which continues to exist but is often supplemented or replaced with webinars. One of the most popular examples of live events that support informal learning is the conference (discussed in chapter 5).

Core Technologies Used in Informal Learning

As computers came into increasingly widespread use in the second half of the last century, training and development professionals saw uses for them in supporting learning activities. The first online learning programs appeared in the late 1960s and early 1970s. The first online help systems, which provided users with instructions on how to use those computers, appeared a decade later. Word processing appeared at about the same time, as did resources to teach and reinforce writing skills, such as online spelling and grammar checkers. Although most workers take these innovations for granted today, their developments represented major milestones in instructional design and learning, and these technologies still provide the foundation for much informal learning.

Such technologies, which use the basic capabilities of computers and have been available for several decades, are central to informal learning online and, therefore, are called *core technologies* for the purposes of this discussion.

The primary characteristics of core technologies are that they permit people to create, store, retrieve, and transmit content, and they promote interaction between learners and instructors. Some people call these web 1.0 technologies. Training and development professionals often overlook the role (and use) of core technologies in informal learning. See Table 7–3 for descriptions of core technologies used in informal learning.

Table 7–3. Core Technologies Used With Informal Learning

Type of Technology	Description
Online informational content	Refers to material published online for explanatory and illustrative purposes, including news, policies and procedures, instructions, reference material, and opinions. This material takes a variety of forms; among the most popular are informative websites, online help, news sites, webzines, online books, user's and troubleshooting guides, and advice columns. This material usually appears in one of these formats: as a traditional webpage, as a guided tour (an animated sequence, like a movie trailer), online help, or a PDF. Training and development professionals create this material using software such as word processors, desktop publishing programs, web authoring programs, and audiovisual editing programs.

(continued)

Table 7–3. Core Technologies Used With Informal Learning (continued)

Databases	Refers to information that is stored in a structured manner in a central location and that users can view in a variety of ways. Databases typically hold essential information, such as customer and supplier lists and product inventories. What distinguishes a database from other types of information is that the information is stored in records, each record has the same type of information, and users can view the information in a way that is meaningful to them. In terms of informal learning, learners often explore databases to discover useful patterns that might suggest future courses of action.
Repositories	Refers to specialized databases of resources that are produced by people from several organizations. In the context of learning, repositories store lessons and teaching resources designed by training and development professionals who hope that their colleagues will also use these materials. Because many of these materials were designed to promote learning, they are called *learning objects*. Some resources are free to use; others require a usage fee.
Email	In terms of informal learning, email serves countless purposes. Among the most common is one person asking another for advice, information, or instruction.
Chat	During electronic chats, all parties are online and communicating at the same time. The chat can occur solely through text as well as through voice and a live video feed. Training and development professionals use instant messaging and Internet telephone programs to chat. In terms of informal learning, chat—like email—has many uses, but among its most common is tutoring of individual learners taking e-learning courses.
Discussion boards and discussion lists	Discussion boards refer to websites that allow users to post questions and other users to respond. Discussion lists operate similarly, but through email. One user emails a question to all who subscribe to the discussion list, and others respond. The technical name for discussion lists is *listservs*. Training and development professionals create discussion boards and lists using software in learning and course management systems. In terms of informal learning, discussion boards and lists let learners continue a discussion that began in a formal class, or bring together people who share a common interest so they can continue their learning.
Podcasts and vodcasts	Refers to audio (podcasts) and video recordings (vodcasts) saved in digital formats. Training and development professionals create this material using a variety of software, from basic recording software included with Windows and Mac, to advanced professional audio and video editing software. In terms of informal learning, training and development professionals tend to use podcasts and vodcasts in two ways: One is similar to classic audio and video recordings; the other is for informal, quickly recorded messages.

Live virtual classroom	Refers to live sessions conducted online, in which all parties are participating at the same time (called *synchronous communication*). In such a presentation, participants can talk with one another, share slides, display their screens to other participants, and chat using text. Sessions can also be recorded. Because these sessions are broadcast over the web, some people call them *webcasts*. Because the sessions are like seminars on the web, other people call them *webinars*. Training and development professionals create webcasts and webinars using virtual meeting or virtual classroom software. In terms of informal learning, people use webinars for lectures, virtual lunch and learns, product updates, online conferences, and virtual chats with leaders, among other things.
E-courses	Courses that have been transferred online from another format such as a classroom or workbook, often with little or no re-imagining of the way that the content is presented. Training and development professionals can transfer classroom courses online by recording narration to accompany existing PowerPoint slides, or cutting and pasting workbook material into a template in an e-learning authoring tool. Because training and development professionals shuttled these courses from one medium to another, they earned the name *shuttleware*. More recently, industry analysts have named this type of e-learning *rapid* or *Level 1 e-learning*. These courses primarily offer information rather than instruction.
E-learning programs	Online courses designed to develop skills. One of the primary differentiators between e-courses and e-learning is that e-learning programs typically include engaging activities that help learners develop skills and assess their capabilities. These activities include simulations, games, role plays, and case studies. Because planning and producing these activities takes additional time and resources, these courses can take two to 10 times longer to develop than e-courses. Industry analysts call them *Level 2* and *Level 3* e-learning to indicate the additional levels of interaction. Training and development professionals create this material using course authoring software like Flash and Dreamweaver, audiovisual production software, and specialized software for simulations and testing.

When considering the relative costs and development times for core media, note that podcasts and vodcasts cost less and require less development time than the audio and video recordings used in classic media. That's because production methods differ and the quality of some digital production methods is lower than traditional methods. In many instances, however, workers accept materials of a lower production quality in digital format than they do in traditional audio and video formats.

Social Media Used in Informal Learning

Social media are web-based tools that let users easily share information, collaborate, and communicate. Admittedly, users could share information, collaborate, and communicate with core technologies, but web 2.0 technologies make it easier, and as a result, encourage greater levels of sharing and interaction.

Basic Rule

When considering a particular technology, think about these issues: the capabilities of the technology, and if they are appropriate for your needs; the cost to acquire and support the technology, as well as to prepare learning experiences that use that technology; the time needed to design, develop, and deliver materials in that technology—some technologies are inexpensive but can use a lot of time (ask some social networking addicts). These practical considerations play a key role in choosing technologies for informal learning.

One of the most significant purposes that social media serve is supporting learning among peers. Like the OpenSpace meeting format, in which everyone brings and shares their expertise, so in social media everyone who participates brings and shares expertise. For a list of social media platforms that support informal learning, see Table 7–4.

Table 7–4. Forms of Social Media Used for Informal Learning

Form of Social Media	Description
Photo and video sharing services	Refers to services that let people publish photos and videos in a central location and make them widely available to others. Training and development professionals create the photos and videos using the same types of software used to create podcasts and vodcasts. In terms of informal learning, training and development professionals can, with permission, use the images in materials they produce. Shared videos and photos provide instruction on a number of common concepts and procedures, such as the extensive collection of how-to videos on YouTube.
Blogs	Although originally conceived as a personal online journal, blogs (shortened form of *web log*) have evolved to become the basis of conversations between an author (called a *blogger*) and readers. Bloggers post entries, and readers respond by posting comments. Training and development professionals create blogs using publicly available software, like Blogger and Wordpress, or with blogging tools built into other software used in their organizations. In terms of informal learning, blogs provide learners with content and opinion-based perspectives. The real discussion—and learning—often occurs in the reader comments that follow a blog entry.

Microblogging	Refers to the 140-character messages that people post using Twitter, and brief status updates on social networking sites like LinkedIn and Facebook. Because Twitter popularized microblogging and each post on this site is called a *tweet*, many people refer to the act of microblogging as *tweeting*. In terms of informal learning, training and development professionals use microblogging to direct users to longer articles and blog posts of possible interest, to report news, and to discuss an event with others, usually while the event is occurring.
Wikis and collaborative applications	Refers to a document that is jointly created by several users. The best known document created with a wiki is Wikipedia, named after the authoring tool. Training and development professionals use specialized software to create wikis. In terms of informal learning, wikis serve as reference materials to which others in the organization can contribute. The documents are viewable by everyone in the organization. A variation on wikis are collaborative applications. These work similarly to wikis in that all users work from a centralized file and can contribute to it, but they differ from wikis in that users can create not only documents, but also spreadsheets and presentations.
Electronic portfolios (e-portfolios)	Refers to a collection of work presented on the web, as well as accompanying reflections that describe how the work was created. E-portfolios sometimes include a self-evaluation of the work, as well as space for peers and advisers to provide comments. Training and development professionals encourage workers to create e-portfolios using a variety of web development software and online templates. In terms of informal learning, the samples included with e-portfolios, as well as the related reflections, provide a means of evaluating competence acquired through informal learning efforts.
Social networking	Refers to websites that let users publish content. Users have personal *networks*, consisting of people whom the users have invited to see their profiles (or who have received such an invitation from another user). User profiles display information about who they are, where they live, what type of work they do, and what interests they have. In addition, social networks let users create "groups" that let people share information with others outside their networks who have a common interest. Training and development professionals can use publicly available software to form social networks, or they can create networks on proprietary software, such as software embedded in Lotus groupware. Many organizations prefer that employees use private networks to prevent the leaking of sensitive information. In terms of informal learning, training and development professionals use social networks to make announcements and similar types of communication and to bring together people who might not otherwise meet.

(continued)

Table 7–4. Forms of Social Media Used for Informal Learning (continued)

Mentor matching	Refers to software that matches mentors and protégés. Mentor-matching software works much like online dating software; potential mentors and protégés complete profiles, and the system matches those who have similar interests. The software also provides a means for possible matches to interact with one another. One of the primary benefits of mentor-matching software is that it promotes mentoring across geographic boundaries. Training and development professionals use specialized software to facilitate mentoring relationships throughout their organizations, especially with protégés who might not find a suitable mentor in their immediate work environments.
Ratings or ranking systems	Refers to software that lets participants rate and comment on products or sevices described on a website. Some popular websites that let participants provide ratings include eBay, Amazon, and TripAdvisor. Other viewers use these opinions and ratings to learn about the product or service. Some enterprise learning software lets users provide opinions and ratings of learning resources, including formal courses, e-learning, and e-courses.
Virtual worlds	Refers to software that provides a three-dimensional (3-D) online environment where users can interact in unscripted ways with others who are online at the same time. 3-D environments can be designed to resemble real environments (like museums and businesses) or imaginary ones, and can be public or private. Training and development professionals create this material using publicly available software like SecondLife, or specialized animation and simulation software. In terms of informal learning, virtual worlds can be a venue for online classes and lectures that let users interact with each other. More significantly, virtual worlds provide an environment for certain types of simulation activities.

One of the most significant benefits of social media is that they simplify production and sharing of content and thus reduce both the cost and time involved. Although the prospect of workers learning from one another through social media offers exciting opportunities, consider a few downsides of the technology.

- ▶ Learning professionals have not extensively integrated social media into their work. Furthermore, many trials using Twitter, Facebook, and blogs for learning have had mixed results, and the issue of sustaining interest was one that arose in many studies.
- ▶ Confusion exists around basic terminology for social media, just as it does for informal learning in general. One common type of confusion is among

blogs and wikis. Blogs are individually written pieces that clearly identify the author and individual commenters on it. In contrast, a wiki is a collaboratively written document; the identity of individual authors is not provided on the screen.

▶ User-provided content might not be accurate. Patti Shank (2008) labels content provided through social media as "buyer beware content." For the most part, the community of contributors eventually ensures that the content will be accurate; studies have shown, for instance, that entries in Wikipedia have a similar level of accuracy to those in the well-regarded *Encyclopedia Brittanica.* However, recently published information may contain inaccuracies that have not yet been weeded out by other contributors.

▶ Etiquette may suffer. Research suggests that people tend to exhibit less-inhibited behavior online than in person and, as a result, are more likely to write inflammatory comments. Concerns about privacy exist. People might inadvertently share sensitive information through social media, perhaps forgetting that these media are public platforms.

One of the most interesting comprehensive examples of social media for informal learning is personalized learning environments (PLEs; Downes, 2006), which are portals that provide workers with links to a variety of informal learning resources. Workers can choose the social media and other resources to which they would like access from their portal or home page. PLEs are still prototypes (that is, in early phases of testing), and mostly are intended for students in primary, secondary, or higher education, rather than adults in the workplace. Still, possibilities exist for learning in the workplace.

Technologies That Facilitate Informal Learning Throughout the Organization

The last category of technologies described in this chapter facilitates informal learning efforts throughout organizations. Although none of the following technologies were designed to address informal learning, some unexpectedly support and facilitate it and other technologies could actually detract from informal learning unless carefully watched. These technologies fall into two groups:

> enterprise learning systems, such as learning management systems (LMSs), learning content management systems (LCMSs), course management systems, and talent management systems, which let organizations strategically choose and distribute learning materials and track their use

> infrastructure—computer controllers, cables, and security, which support or hinder the distribution of content for informal learning.

Enterprise Learning Systems Used With Informal Learning

Enterprise learning systems comprise software and hardware that support the design, development, and delivery of learning programs in an organization *(enterprise)*. These systems also keep records on the programs and transfer information to other systems used in the organization, such as delivering an email message to a manager when a worker completes an e-learning program.

Although originally designed to complement formal learning, different types of enterprise learning systems have capabilities that are useful for specific aspects of informal learning. For example, some enterprise systems let users create and track career development plans, while others provide learners with access to materials for informal learning.

Think About This

Take time to learn about the capabilities of your enterprise learning systems for informal learning. You may be missing out on informal learning opportunities afforded by systems that are already well established at your organization.

Enterprise learning systems encompass five types of software applications. Each has its primary use, although in their secondary uses, many of these systems have overlapping purposes. That overlap can create confusion among training and development professionals. A description of enterprise learning systems used in informal learning can be found in Table 7–5.

Table 7–5. Types of Enterprise Learning Systems Used With Informal Learning

Type of System	Description
Learning management systems (LMSs)	Originally designed for the workplace and intended to automate many of the administrative functions involved in managing courses and training and development groups. LMSs specifically automate enrollment in classroom and online courses, provide automatic reminders about upcoming class sessions, and record grades and report them to stakeholders, as well as share them with other systems. LMSs let instructors and students communicate with one another, and many also provide course catalogs and related career-planning materials. Some LMSs even have capabilities for assessing skills.
Course management systems	Originally designed for the academic environment and intended to support classroom courses. Course management systems let instructors provide syllabi, handouts, and other resources to learners, give and collect assignments, and even administer tests. Course management systems also let students and faculty members communicate with one another online, as a class or in groups. Because these systems facilitate communication among learners in a community as well as the distribution of learning materials, they are useful for informal learning. **Note:** Because the acronym CMS would apply to two types of enterprise systems described here, I am trying to avoid confusion by not using the acronym CMS.
Learning content management systems (LCMSs)	Designed for the workplace environment to store, organize, retrieve, and present electronic learning materials, such as individual lessons, brief passages, videos, and illustrations. LCMSs were specifically designed for organizations that planned to create large repositories of content for e-learning and use much of that content in two or more e-learning programs. As a result, LCMSs store information about the programs that can pass information about the performance of individual learners from one e-learning module to another, and can operate using many LMSs and course management systems that follow the same technical standards.
Content management systems	Designed to help organizations track and manage all of the content they produce, such as reports, plans, policies and procedures, memos, newsletters, references, and user's guides. They help organizations manage content development, keep track of different versions of the content, automate the process of approving content before publication, and facilitate the reuse of content, such as using the same product description on a website and in a brochure. The only type of content they do not easily track is learning modules. Many communications and product information groups use content management systems. In terms of informal learning, much of the content that training and development professionals hope to use in informal learning is stored on content management systems rather than LCMSs.

(continued)

Table 7–5. Types of Enterprise Learning Systems Used With Informal Learning (continued)

Talent management systems	Designed to link together various human resource tasks, including hiring, skills management, training, and performance planning and evaluation. Talent management systems provide templates for creating and monitoring performance and career development plans, as well as reminders about and advice for conducting appraisals. Some talent management systems let managers and human resources staff evaluate skill bases and use that information to determine individual and group needs for learning. Some talent management systems also integrate all of the capabilities of LMSs. The career development and skills assessment capabilities are especially useful in informal learning.

Perhaps the most complex challenge of using enterprise systems lies not in the technology itself, but in its application to real workplaces. Many enterprise systems have far more capabilities than most organizations use. For example, many LMSs and talent management systems can help organizations assess the skills of workers, link those skills to jobs, and assess the extent to which those skills were actually used in jobs. But most organizations do not use these capabilities, either because doing so requires significant changes to their current performance planning and evaluation processes, which they are hesitant to undertake, or because they are unaware of them.

Infrastructure for Informal Learning

An *infrastructure* refers to the hardware and software that run typical organizational computer networks and connect workers to learning opportunities. The infrastructure also includes the controls and processes employed to make sure that the networks run smoothly. When the infrastructure works well, it works invisibly—both to the workers and to the learning professionals who use the network to make informal learning opportunities available.

At the heart of a network are servers, where organizations store content as well as the programs that facilitate communications, such as email and social networking. Networks usually have several servers; different programs are physically housed on different servers. Linking to the servers are devices such as computers, tablets, and smartphones, which use the content and programs stored on the servers.

Basic Rule

Before finalizing plans to use a technology for informal learning, speak with the information technology specialists in your organization to make sure that the infrastructure can support the plans. Video, audio, social networking, and highly interactive programs often challenge the bandwidth (capacity) of the network. Linking to external sites raises security concerns. As a result, either the learning programs or other software might not run properly. Checking as early as possible helps avoid disappointment closer to the launch of the informal learning event.

Connections between servers and devices occur through telecommunications. Telecommunications consists of physical connections among servers and devices—whether through telephone lines, cables, satellite transmissions, or a combination of these—as well as the software that sends messages and materials from one device or server to others.

Some types of informal learning materials, such as learning programs that use video, live voice connections, animation, and rich simulations, require higher capacity networks and telecommunications links to work well. Using such resources on networks not equipped to support them can cause network-wide slowdowns called *performance problems* (not to be confused with problems of human performance). As a result, information technology staffs often try to avoid resources that require high-capacity networks in an effort to prevent such slowdowns.

Other organizations limit access to outside websites for fear of security problems. For example, some organizations prevent workers from using Facebook onsite because of concerns that Facebook software provides others with unauthorized access to these private networks.

In some instances, providing informal learning opportunities requires changes to the technology infrastructure. Most organizations have a *governance* process that suggests how to request such changes, the standards and guidelines that changes must adhere to, and the approvals required to make the changes.

Getting It Done

This chapter has offered some practical ways to use social media in informal learning. Table 7–6 serves as a summary of the technologies described in this chapter. Worksheet 7–1 offers an opportunity for some practical application practice.

Table 7–6. Technologies Used with the Different Types of Informal Learning Activities

Devices Used for Informal Learning	
Audiovisual equipment	Computers
Printed matter	Tablets
E-book readers	Mobile devices
Classic Media Used With Informal Learning	
Printed matter	Audio recordings
Live events, such as lectures, exhibitions, meetings, and conferences	Videos
Core Technologies Used With Informal Learning	
Online informational content	Discussion boards and discussion lists
Databases	Podcasts and vodcasts
Repositories	Live virtual classroom
Email	E-courses
Chat	E-learning programs
Forms of Social Media Used for Informal Learning	
Photo and video sharing services	Social networking
Blogs	Mentor matching
Microblogging	Ratings or ranking systems
Wikis and collaborative applications	Virtual worlds
Electronic portfolios (e-portfolios)	
Enterprise Learning Systems Used With Informal Learning	
Learning management systems (LMSs)	Content management systems
Course management systems	Talent management systems
Learning content management systems (LCMSs)	

Worksheet 7–1. Exercises

How might you use technology to provide informal learning opportunities in your organization? Try these exercises to find out.

1. As part of an initiative to encourage staff to develop an awareness of business issues, you want to make available online copies of the top 10 bestselling business books as well as subscriptions to five of the most popular weekly and monthly business magazines. To save costs, you plan to offer the materials electronically. And to encourage workers to reflect on what they have read and how they might integrate it into their work, you also plan to offer an online book club.

    What technologies might you use for this undertaking?

    _____

    _____

    _____

    _____

    _____

    Debriefing of exercise 1: A variety of hardware and software technologies help launch this endeavor:

    - For providing workers with access to the online books and magazines, you might make use of e-book software. You could provide them with tablet computers, devices which would not only let them read the materials, but also participate in the book club. Magazines can be viewed on the web with appropriate subscriptions. Some publications have specialized applications (called *apps*) for viewing issues on tablets and smartphones.

    - You might also use a social networking application for facilitating book club discussions. Before starting the book club, make sure that the workers can use the social networking software inside your offices.

2. To help workers for a large tax accounting firm keep up-to-date with new tax laws, a team in the organization is designing and developing a central website that all workers in the organization can check to find out which changes have occurred to the tax code and how these changes affect their work. But the senior vice president for tax accounting is concerned that most workers will forget to use the website.

    What technologies can you use to make the website a go-to place in the organization?

    _____

    _____

    _____

    _____

    _____

Debriefing of exercise 2: The senior vice president probably has good reason to be concerned that the site alone will not keep workers informed. The additional use of the following technologies, most of which can be integrated into the website, can help make it a go-to place for workers:

- Email, microblogging, and similar technologies can inform workers about changes to the tax code that might interest them and direct workers to the website for more details.

- Blogs on the site can summarize developments by topic area and provide perspective on the changes.

- A wiki, where experts in particular aspects of the tax code can provide in-depth information about the implications of particular changes in the tax code.

- Live virtual classrooms can be used for occasional live events that announce complex changes and let workers ask experts about the implications of these changes.

- Articles on the website can provide information about specific tax code changes.

- Social networking provides a place where groups of workers who have an interest in a particular aspect of the tax code can hold open discussions about recent changes and their impact.

- A repository can provide updated tax forms.

Technology can be helpful in reaching workers. But if these platforms are not easily accessible or are filled with outdated information, workers won't use them for their learning needs. As noted in chapter 4, maintaining content is as important as the technology used to distribute it within the organization.

8

How to Evaluate Informal Learning

What's Inside This Chapter

In this chapter, you'll learn

▶ why evaluation of informal learning differs from formal learning
▶ a framework for evaluating informal learning
   ▶ techniques for evaluating informal learning at the individual level
   ▶ techniques for evaluating informal learning across groups of workers
▶ unique issues in reporting evaluations of informal learning.

Curtis, the site supervisor for a construction firm, double- and triple-checks policies and procedures to make sure he's operating within his authority after losing an earlier job because he failed to do so. Losing that job shook Curtis's self-confidence, and even though he has studied the management policies and procedures of his new employer closely and consults them frequently, he still feels that he does not know them. Curtis's manager, however, has noticed that when Curtis speaks to her about work situations, he uses the language of the policies and procedures in his conversation. For example, when discussing safety procedures for noisy areas, Curtis uses the term "hearing protection," which is used in the policies and procedures manual, rather than "ear plugs," which is more commonly used on the floor. Similarly, she recently overheard Curtis advise one of his workers that he's due for an annual hearing test—a week before the notices were sent by human resources. These signs suggest that Curtis has learned a lot about management policies and procedures in this organization.

Determining what workers have learned informally, the extent to which they learned it, and how they apply it are three fundamental questions that arise with informal learning. Similarly important questions concern the impact of learning activities, materials, and support provided by training and development professionals and others in the organization. Answering these questions is the purpose of evaluation, the last of the considerations for integrating informal learning into the workplace.

This chapter explores the evaluation of informal learning. It begins by explaining why evaluation is important, yet why you need to forget most of what you know about evaluation of formal learning when evaluating *in*formal learning. Then, after explaining what you can't do, it presents a framework of what you can do to evaluate informal learning.

How Evaluation of Formal and Informal Learning Differ

Training and development professionals evaluate learning programs for three primary reasons: to assess effectiveness (that is, to determine the extent to which a particular program or set of materials achieved their objectives); to determine whether learning has occurred; and to provide accountability (to demonstrate that the resources invested in learning programs have been responsibly used). For many professionals in this field, the ultimate expression of accountability involves demonstrating a return on investment (ROI), which shows not only that the learners have mastered the skills and knowledge presented in the training programs, but also that in doing so, the organization has realized a benefit that exceeds the cost of the training program.

Underlying this interest in evaluation is the assumption that training and development professionals have the primary responsibility for designing, developing, and implementing the learning program. But this assumption does not underlie informal learning. As noted earlier in this book, informal learning experiences are not always designed; they are often unplanned, impromptu extensions of work projects or supplemental lessons of formal learning programs.

One of the reasons for this is that workers themselves often have primary responsibility for informal learning; they identify what they need to learn, how to learn it, and whether they succeeded. For the most part, training and development professionals support this informal learning by making sure that workers have access to appropriate resources when the need arises and are supported in their efforts to learn. But most informal learning occurs without the direct involvement of training and development professionals.

These differences in the nature of formal and informal learning result in different issues driving evaluation. While measuring learning and its impact drives evaluation of formal learning, merely figuring out whether people learned anything at all and what they learned often drives the evaluation of informal learning. Researcher Victoria Marsick (Marsick and Watkins, 2011) labels the task "surfacing the learning."

As a result of these differences, Donald Kirkpatrick's (1994) four-level framework for evaluating training programs, which is the de facto standard for evaluating formal training programs among training and development professionals, does not provide an adequate framework for evaluating informal learning. Table 8–1 identifies challenges for evaluating informal learning in each of the four levels of the Kirkpatrick methodology.

Table 8–1. Challenges of Using the Kirkpatrick Methodology to Evaluate Informal Learning

Level	Issue
Reaction (Level 1)	Assesses learners' reactions to a formal learning event designed by a training and development professional. Nearly all informal learning programs, however, are designed (at least in part) by the workers themselves for their unique needs at the time. So this level would evaluate workers' satisfaction with their own customized, one-use-only learning program—assuming the worker was even aware that learning happened at all.
Learning (Level 2)	Assesses the extent to which learners achieved the observable and measurable objectives that a third party established for the learning program. In informal learning, workers establish their own objectives for learning, so learning must be assessed on a case-by-case basis. In many instances, objectives are not easily observable and measurable. One reason for this is that objectives for many informal programs fall into the *affective* or motivational realm, where assessment techniques still lack the rigor of those used for assessing learning in the psychomotor (physical skills) and cognitive (intellectual) domains. Also, informal learning often occurs incidentally or unconsciously, so much of it lacks formal objectives against which to measure. Even if training and development professionals could determine what learning to evaluate, because it often occurs in the context of everyday work activities, stopping to conduct a test of learning seems inappropriately disruptive.
Behavior or Transfer (Level 3)	Assesses the extent to which learners applied the lessons from training on the job. Like Level 2 evaluation, transfer is rooted in the learning objectives, but as just noted, much informal learning lacks formal objectives against which to measure. When objectives exist, they vary widely among workers based on their individual needs. As a result, training and development professionals would have difficulty devising standard measures of transfer to track.
Impact (including ROI) (Level 4)	Assesses the benefits from investing in a training program. To assess impact, training and development professionals must first establish the business objectives of the program. In most cases, however, an organization has no specific business objective in mind for particular informal learning efforts. Rather, organizations seek benefit from their overall support of a particular type of informal learning. For example, by providing comprehensive support for career development activities, an organization might contain recruiting and turnover costs. Although research has demonstrated that such links exist, it has not shown that actual financial benefits always accrue by offering training (Tharenou, Saks, and Moore, 2007).

Basic Rule

The Kirkpatrick framework and related methodologies are incompatible with informal learning and therefore cannot be used for evaluating this type of workplace learning.

A Framework for Evaluating Informal Learning

With different questions guiding evaluation and without formal objectives and criterion-referenced tests, how do training and development professionals evaluate informal learning? Effective evaluation of learning programs starts with clear questions. Methods merely provide a means for collecting the data that answers those questions. The questions guiding the evaluation of informal learning include:

▶ What did workers learn informally?

▶ How do workers learn informally?

▶ How can workers receive recognition for their informal learning?

▶ What is the extent of participation in various informal learning activities?

▶ What is the extent of satisfaction with various resources used for informal learning?

▶ In what ways does the organization benefit from informal learning by workers?

▶ Which informal learning efforts that the organization formally supports are providing tangible benefits to the organization?

▶ How can organizations better support informal learning efforts?

A closer look at these questions suggests that some of them focus on learning at the individual level, while others help evaluate learning across groups of workers. Table 8–2 suggests a way to organize specific evaluation issues in these two categories—individual learning and learning across groups—to create a framework of evaluation for informal learning. The next sections explore each part of this framework in depth and suggest at least one activity (and often more) you can undertake at each level to evaluate informal learning.

Table 8–2. A Model for Evaluating Informal Learning

Individual Learning	Learning Across Groups of Workers
Identify *what* workers learned, using these evaluation methods: • Self-assessments • Process portfolios • Coaching interviews	Determine the extent to which individual resources for informal learning were used, using these evaluation methods: • Analytics • Compiling data from evaluations of individual learning efforts
Identify *how* workers learned it, using these evaluation methods: • Process portfolios • Coaching	Assess satisfaction with individual resources, using these evaluation methods: • Surveys • Focus groups
Recognize acquired competencies, using these evaluation methods: • Employee education records • Skills assessments • Certifications • Badges	Identify the impact of individual resources, using these evaluation methods: • Rater systems • Specialized reports • Long-term studies

Basic Rule
Evaluating informal learning involves first assessing learning at the individual level and then exploring broader patterns in learning to determine how to best support it in the future.

Evaluating Individual Learning

As noted earlier, learning that happens as a result of individual initiative or serendipitous activity is difficult to identify, much less label and report. Getting at this information involves

▶ **Identifying what workers have learned.** Because workers establish their own objectives for some informal learning and other informal learning occurs unconsciously—and without objectives—often neither the workers themselves nor training and development professionals are aware of what individual workers have learned. This type of evaluation helps unearth what learning occurred.

▶ **Identifying how workers have learned.** Training and development professionals can use this type of evaluation to find out whether the resources provided for informal learning were actually used, and if not, find out which resources were used instead and why.

▶ **Recognizing acquired competencies.** This type of evaluation lets employers label the skills, knowledge, and abilities learned by workers, and formally acknowledge it in employees' education records. Such formal acknowledgment is useful when assigning job tasks or deciding on raises and promotions. This recognition also motivates workers to continue their informal learning efforts because it provides them with a tangible "credit" for individual activities often undertaken without anyone's involvement or awareness.

Training and development professionals use the following evaluation methods to gather information about individual learning that occurs informally.

Self-assessments are instruments that workers use to assess the extent to which they have learned material in a particular domain. In many ways, self-assessments are like quizzes, in that they involve answering a series of questions or demonstrating a skill and then receiving feedback on performance. Self-assessments work best for identifying *what* workers have learned in domains that are well defined, or for content that has been externally defined.

With self-assessments, however, workers generally administer the "test" on their own, and the results are intended to reflect what workers have learned and where they need to continue their efforts. The results may or may not be recorded.

Effective formal self-assessments usually

▶ assess objectives that would be covered in a formal training program on the subject

▶ focus on how workers might respond to various work-related situations, so that the self-assessment seems relevant and engaging to them

▶ provide correct answers to questions and then explain why the answer was correct, so workers can learn from the experience.

The activity at the end of chapter 1 ("Are You an Informal Learner?") is an example of a self-assessment that follows these guidelines.

For broader skills that cannot be addressed in a simple written assessment, responses tend to focus on distinctions in ways of thinking—such as a worker who has fully integrated the learning, a worker who has partially integrated the learning, and a worker who has not yet integrated the learning.

Process portfolios are collections of work accompanied by reflections and commentary about how the worker created the work samples, what the worker learned in the process of doing so, and how he or she felt about the learning process (Carliner, 2005). Portfolios are usually created in collaboration with the worker's manager, mentor, or another senior colleague.

The portfolio is called a *process portfolio* because its primary focus is on the means by which workers created the work samples. Portfolios grow with time and provide workers with opportunities to reflect not only on individual assignments but also on learning and development that occurred over time. They are often used in career development and counseling discussions.

A process portfolio contrasts with the better-known *showcase portfolio*, which highlights workers' best work and merely states how they contributed to a project, rather than what they learned from it. Workers use showcase portfolios to provide evidence of qualifications for a position.

There are two components to a process portfolio, in which the worker provides commentary on his or her work samples. Figure 8–1 presents the template for the first part of the commentary. Workers use this part of the commentary in both process and showcase portfolios. It provides general information about the project and their contribution to it. Figure 8–2 presents the template for the second part of the commentary—specific information about workers' professional development in the context of a project. Workers use this part of the commentary only in process portfolios; it is separated so that workers can easily create showcase portfolios from the same materials used to create the process portfolios. The templates can be adapted for different types of work assignments.

Figure 8–1. Template for the First Part of the Commentary for a Process Portfolio—General Information About a Project and Workers' Contributions to It

Title	
Type of Program	
Client	
Production Tools Used	(Only provide the relevant information. If something does not apply, do not include it.) Authoring tool: Graphics tool: Animation tool: Learning management system: Learning content management system: Content management system:
About This Sample	In 100 words or less, describe the purpose and audience of the sample.
Unique Issues	Using bullets, list as many as five issues or challenges faced when developing this course.
Your Contributions	In 100 words or less, describe the contributions you made and the assistance you received.

Figure 8–2. Template for the Second Part of the Commentary—Specific Information About Workers' Professional Development During a Project and Their Feelings About It

In your own words, what was the purpose of this assignment?	
Which skills were you supposed to develop through this project?	
Which skills were you already good at? How could you demonstrate that?	
Which skills did you need for this project? What specifically did you need to learn? How did you learn it? How do you feel about your ability to demonstrate this skill?	

(continued)

Figure 8–2. Template for the Second Part of the Commentary (continued)

What was the most challenging aspect of this project?	
What was the most fun?	
How confident do you feel about your ability to handle a project like this on your own? How many tries would you need before getting the assignment right? Why do you feel this way? What could further build your confidence?	
What are the three most significant lessons you'll take away from this project in your work?	1. 2. 3.
What are the next steps you are planning to take to strengthen the skills addressed by this assignment?	

The two parts of the commentary help to elicit lessons informally through a project. The discussion of the role and tools used to develop the project, for example, help workers identify what they knew starting the project and what they learned as a result of working on it (Teja, 2011).

Process portfolios can help training and development professionals determine *how* workers learned in addition to helping identify *what* workers learned. In particular, when responding to the second part of the commentary, some workers might identify parts of the process that provided learning opportunities. This commentary also asks workers to share their feelings about the learning process so that those reviewing the portfolio gain insights into the feelings of support and frustration the worker felt.

Coaching interviews with managers, mentors, senior workers, and similarly experienced and trained co-workers provide learners with the opportunity to get a second opinion on their learning processes. An effective coach helps workers gain a realistic perspective on the extent of their learning, not only asking workers to state what they have learned, but also asking them to provide concrete evidence that demonstrates that learning actually occurred.

In some instances, workers might not believe that they learned anything at all. By actively listening to workers, however, coaches might gain an alternate perspective. For example, a worker might not feel that he or she learned anything on the job or through a developmental experience, but then display knowledge that would not have been intuitive—and could only have resulted from the learning experiences. The coach uses these clues to suggest that learning has indeed occurred.

Coaching also provides an opportunity to explore *how* learning occurred after identifying what workers learned. To find out how workers learned, coaches should specifically ask workers about critical incidents in the work process, identifying what occurred at each of these junctures and then exploring how workers felt about these learning opportunities.

Employee education records track training completed by employees. Organizations use this information to acknowledge skills maintained and added. Nearly all large organizations and many medium and small organizations keep these records.

Most organizations have established ways of automatically crediting workers for completing classroom, self-study, and virtual e-learning programs by tracking these through learning management systems, which transfer the information to employee education records.

Other information must be entered manually into the employee education record, such as completions of training offered by third-party providers, completion of academic courses, and completions of informal learning efforts. Organizational policies vary on who can update records and the evidence that must accompany the updated records. Some organizations let workers update their own education records and operate on an honor system. Others only let managers or human resources specialists update records and require that workers provide concrete evidence of completions.

Skills assessments are another means of recognizing informal learning by crediting workers for developing skills partially or completely through informal means. Many learning management systems provide the capability for tracking skills, but few organizations actually take advantage of this capability. That's because most skills assessments involve rating workers on a list of specific skills that often exceeds 100 items. Some of the skills on these lists are general ones that apply to all jobs, such as the ability to work cooperatively with others and the ability to use common software applications, like word processing, spreadsheets, and email. Other skills are specific to a class of jobs, such as skills associated with litigation and managing intellectual property among legal advisers, and the skills associated with providing technical support and correcting software problems among information technology professionals.

Although some skills assessment schemes ask people to rate skills in general terms, such as excellent, very good, or poor, more effective skills assessment schemes use rating schemes based on concrete and observable measures, such as "I have never heard of this skill," "I can describe this skill but have never demonstrated it," "I have demonstrated this skill once or twice," "I have demonstrated this skill three or more times," and "I advise others on how to acquire this skill." This prevents workers from under- and over-rating their skills.

Skills assessment efforts face these challenges:

- ▶ Identification of skills. Some organizations choose to identify and assess broad skills, which often fail to provide specific information. Others identify highly specific skills, but the lists become so long (some exceeding 150 skills) that the assessments are too time-consuming and intellectually exhausting to complete.
- ▶ Self-reported data, usually entered by the worker with little or no verification. A second evaluation from a manager helps, but it is still opinion-based data.
- ▶ Timeliness, because the skills assessment represents the list of skills identified in a particular worker at a particular point in time. Some skills may atrophy with disuse, and workers may have acquired other skills that will not be reflected unless they have updated their skills assessments.

Certifications are another valuable evaluation tool for recognizing competencies. Workers demonstrate their competency through one or more of these means:

- passing examinations that demonstrate familiarity with a body of knowledge central to the field
- demonstrating competencies according to criteria identified and assessed by external assessors
- preparing a portfolio for evaluation by external assessors, that validates the originality of the work and provides evidence of competency to perform the work.

Although to be eligible for some certification exams, workers must have completed required formal training, the certification exam itself focuses on competence, regardless of how workers actually acquired it. As a result, certifications recognize informal learning by providing external, third-party recognition of skills and knowledge developed partially or completely through informal means.

Certifications are offered by several groups: professional and trade associations, who usually certify competence in a profession; technology providers, who usually certify the ability to competently install, use, or repair a machine or software; and internally within organizations to certify the ability to perform a job that is vital to the organization.

Learning badges are another type of recognition offered by some websites and independent learning organizations (such as the open courses at MIT) that provide external verification that a participant has completed a particular learning activity, and identify the skill that the learner has acquired. Learning badges are a relatively new development (announced as this book was going to press), so their impact on the evaluation of informal learning is not yet known.

Additional ways to evaluate and recognize individual learning exist. For details, check the *European Guidelines for Validating Non-formal and Informal Learning* published on the web by the European Centre for the Development of Vocational Training (CEDEFOP).

Learning Across Groups of Workers

Although evaluating individual efforts to learn informally helps individual workers identify what they have learned and receive recognition for it, it does not provide insights into broader informal learning patterns across all workers in the organization, much less the extent or impact of those efforts. Only a second category of evaluations can determine whether organization-wide efforts to support informal learning are having an impact, and which efforts provide the most benefit, which provide the least, and where opportunity exists to strengthen support.

This second category of evaluation techniques provides these insights. These evaluations consider informal learning across groups of workers and specifically focus on:

> ▸ **Determining the extent to which individual resources are used.** One of the first challenges of evaluating learning across groups of workers is determining which resources they are consulting—and which ones they're avoiding. Analytics and compiling data from evaluations of individual learning efforts provide data to address this issue.

> ▸ **Assessing satisfaction with individual resources.** Training and development professionals can use this information to provide more satisfying informal learning resources and experiences in the future. Two types of evaluations solicit general information about satisfaction with informal learning resources: surveys and focus groups.

> ▸ **Identifying the impact of individual resources.** This type of evaluation assesses whether these resources are collectively making a difference among workers. Three methods intended to identify the impact of resources are rater systems, specialized reports, and long-term studies.

Training and development professionals use the following evaluation methods to gather information about learning that occurs across groups of workers.

Analytics refers to the reports provided by information systems that contain statistics on the use of various online resources, including those that are typically used for informal learning, such as self-study courses, online manuals, and websites. Such statistics reveal the number of workers who use these resources as well as the extent to which they do so.

No single system is likely to provide reports on all of the online resources for informal learning. Learning management systems only provide reports on materials made available through these systems. Typically, these include tutorials, webinars, face-to-face events requiring preregistration (such as a lecture), related resources such as job aids, and online discussions associated with these events, including discussions occurring through discussion boards and email messages.

But much informal learning that occurs online involves the use of resources that were not intended for learning, nor posted through a learning management system. In light of this, many organizations post and track websites using either their enterprise content management system or Google Analytics (tools provided by Google for tracking use of websites).

Other statistics are provided through social networking. When organizations use private social networking software to connect people inside the organization, rather than generally available social networking platforms like LinkedIn and Twitter, they can also generate reports that describe the use of those networks.

Although the information might come from several sources, the nature of the information needed is often similar across systems and types of content. Here's a breakdown of the type of information provided through analytics:

- Number of uses. How many times were the online materials accessed? Most systems can provide information on access to individual pages rather than just to the website, so training and development professionals can see which parts of a website are more widely used than others.
- Number of unique users. This identifies the number of people who visited a page, whether the person visited the page one or 100 times. Identifying the number of unique users helps put the number of uses into perspective, revealing whether single users typically visited several times or users typically visit a page just once.
- Extent of use, or how long people stayed on the webpage. Some web experts call this *stickiness*, assuming that people who stay on a webpage for a long time feel engaged with it. But another explanation exists; people might have switched to another session on their computer without closing the page. In such instances, the analytics show that the page was in use, when in actuality, the user did not even look at it most of the time.

Although analytics may provide facts about the use of online resources for informal learning, they cannot explain why workers choose to use certain resources and abandon others, and they cannot indicate workers' satisfaction with these resources.

Compiling data from evaluations of individual learning efforts involves looking at patterns of usage and behavior among the portfolios, coaching notes, skills assessments, and certifications compiled in the evaluation of individual learning efforts. In other words, you are taking an inventory of learning methods and content from these resources. This inventory might explore how workers learned through individual efforts (like reading, taking self-study courses, and experimentation) and collaborative efforts (such as mentoring and work projects).

Although each worker usually sets his or her own unique learning goals and chooses how to learn, similarities in objectives and methods will likely exist among workers. For example, several workers might have learned how to perform certain technical procedures through coaching from a more experienced worker, even though formal courses exist on those procedures. This could prompt training and development professionals to find out why workers prefer this method to the already available formal course. Figure 8–3 suggests a template you can use to start such an inventory.

Because learners rarely track the time they spend on these activities and lack resources to measure their effectiveness, such an inventory cannot provide definitive data on the success of informal learning efforts. Furthermore, because portfolios and coaching tend to focus on learning as it relates to particular projects, this type of inventory could overlook certain types of informal learning, especially those not related to a current work project.

Even with this limitation, however, such an inventory provides insights into some of the informal learning processes in the organization that might not have been easily uncovered through other means.

Surveys are tools meant to quickly and unobtrusively collect data about satisfaction with informal learning resources. Two types of surveys provide insights into satisfaction with informal learning: those focused on individual resources and those focused on broader informal learning processes.

Figure 8–3. Template From Which to Start an Inventory of Topics and Methods of Informal Learning

Topic Areas (based on specific phase in life span of the job)	Objective (to be added, based on needs of the particular job)	Conscious of Learning or Not?	Individual Learning				Group Learning			
			Method 1	Method 2	Method 3	Method 4	Method 5	Method 6	Method 7	Method 8
Orientation										
Resource 1										
Resource 2										
Onboarding										
Resource 1										
Resource 2										
Building proficiency										
Resource 1										
Resource 2										
Addressing undocumented issues										
Resource 1										
Resource 2										

(continued)

Figure 8–3. Template From Which to Start an Inventory of Topics and Methods of Informal Learning (continued)

Topic Areas (based on specific phase in life span of the job)	Objective (to be added, based on needs of the particular job)	Conscious of Learning or Not?	Individual Learning					Group Learning			
			Method 1	Method 2	Method 3	Method 4	Method 5	Method 6	Method 7	Method 8
Updating skills											
Resource 1											
Resource 2											
Choosing the next job or career											
Resource 1											
Resource 2											
Preparing for the next job or career											
Resource 1											
Resource 2											
Addressing ongoing initiatives											
Resource 1											
Resource 2											

Surveys focusing on individual resources are useful when organizations seek feedback on web-based material that serves an instructional purpose. Figure 8–4 provides a template for feedback that can be placed on individual webpages created to provide user assistance.

Figure 8–4. Template for Feedback on Instructional Webpages

Did this page answer your question?

□   **Yes**

□   **No**

If no, what information did you seek that was not provided?

_____

Organizations can use such specific, targeted feedback to strengthen individual pages of their online content. However, my research suggests that response rates are low and that users who have difficulty with the online content tend to respond more frequently than those who felt that the content was helpful to them, so the feedback received can be a bit one-sided.

Training and development professionals should also seek feedback on satisfaction with resources created for managers and other coaches to support workers in the learning process. Such surveys might ask managers and other coaches these questions:

▶ Did they use the materials? Why or why not?

▶ Did they follow the guidance provided? Why or why not?

▶ Did they feel the guidance was complete? If not, what could be added?

Surveys focusing on broader informal learning processes can include employee opinion surveys or customer surveys. Organizations might conduct an employee opinion survey to get a sense about which aspects of the workplace are satisfactory, which ones need attention, and how engaged employees feel with the organization. Specifically, employee opinion surveys might explore these issues concerning informal learning:

▶ Awareness. The survey might ask workers about their awareness of specific programs offered, such as mentoring, self-study e-learning courses, and lecture series, as well as perceptions about the appropriateness of workers' use of work time to learn informally.

▶ Participation. The survey might ask about workers' participation in a variety of activities intended for informal learning, as well as the extent to which they feel they can learn from existing job assignments and activities (like meetings).

▶ Satisfaction. The survey might ask workers about the extent to which they feel the organization supports not only formal learning efforts, but also the need to learn outside the classroom and on work time.

Customer surveys play a similar role to employee surveys in that they assess customer perceptions of, and satisfaction with, the entire customer experience. Some organizations do not have customers, nor do they sell products and services; but they serve external constituencies and provide them with support for informal learning before and during use of the service. Training and development professionals who work in such situations might adapt the customer survey to this type of situation.

Focus groups are structured conversations with a limited number of people (usually eight to 12 per group) that provide rich insights into particular situations. Focus groups can address the same types of issues as employee and customer surveys, except that the responses are open rather than selected from a predetermined list of items, as is typical on surveys. Furthermore, because the facilitators and participants are meeting at the same time, facilitators can ask participants to clarify and expand on their responses if they believe that doing so might shed additional light on an issue raised.

Some organizations use a combination of focus groups and surveys to gather information on learning processes. They start by conducting focus groups, which provide descriptive information about an aspect of informal learning. As part of the analysis of the focus group, facilitators identify patterns that seem to dominate the discussion. Using those patterns to form the basis of questions for a survey provides organizations with an opportunity to determine whether the patterns were limited to the participants in the focus group or apply to many members of the organization.

Rater systems provide workers with a means of rating the usefulness of various online resources for informal learning. Typical rater systems let users rate the quality of resources from five stars (outstanding or extremely useful) to one star (poor or of little to no use). Any worker who registers with the rater system can provide an assessment; most systems also let workers explain the reasons for their assessment.

Rater systems are best known among online retailers. For example, Amazon.com lets customers rate products, and TripAdvisor.com lets users rate hotels and other tourist attractions and services. But professionals also use rater systems. For example, the eServer for Technical Communication—an online repository of articles about professional and technical communication—lets users rate each article, and MERLOT—an online repository of resources for teaching in schools and colleges—also lets users rate each resource. Some learning and content management systems let workers rate courses and informal learning materials, too.

Specialized reports assess the impact of individual resources or groups of materials. Gathering these specialized reports primarily involves collecting information from different evaluations in a single place.

A single report on the impact of individual resources should probably focus on a limited number of resources—particularly those of high interest. For example, suppose the organization invested in a mentoring program. The evaluation might just focus on the impact of the mentoring program. Or a human resources department might have produced several hundred resources for informal learning about personnel policies and procedures, and might be interested in learning which ones had the most impact. Such a report might identify the most useful resources (and would start by defining what the report means by *useful*, such as the resources receiving the highest evaluations or the ones used most frequently by workers, or some formula that encompasses the two).

The report would combine information about the extent of use, responses to surveys about the items, and ratings of the resources, as well as answers to broader questions about awareness of, and satisfaction with, broader informal learning processes. If workers provide permission to share quotes from individual evaluations, the report might be supplemented with this descriptive information about how particular resources have made an impact on individual workers.

Long-term studies follow the learning journeys of workers over a sustained period of time (anywhere from two to 10 years or longer). At various intervals during that time, these studies report on the progress of that learning journey and the impact that learning has made thus far.

One way of doing this might be to ask workers involved in the study to prepare a process portfolio or to participate in a series of coaching sessions with a training and development professional. Both approaches are intended to "surface the learning" and learning processes. But rather than focusing on learning in a particular assignment, the evaluations of the portfolios or coaching discussions would focus on all learning related to the job, both formal and informal. Training and development professionals would review the portfolios or conduct coaching conversations with all workers in the study at certain milestones, such as the one-, two-, and five-year service anniversaries. The evolving story about these workers provides insights into learning processes at the organization and the impact of this learning on a personal level. It would not indicate a return on investment.

What About ROI?

Although the evaluation methods just described let you report some numerical data about informal learning programs, they do not provide a means for determining the return on investment (ROI) of informal learning.

Sometimes training and development professionals can use program evaluation techniques to assess returns on certain structured efforts provided through informal learning, such as new employee orientation and onboarding and mentoring. But most informal learning efforts defy the techniques used in formal training and program evaluations. Part of the challenge is that calculating the initial investment for many informal learning efforts is nearly impossible. As noted several times in this book, much informal learning starts when a worker recognizes a need within the scope of a work assignment, or it happens unconsciously, when the worker is focused on some other activity. The learning has no official beginning or end, nor does it have well-defined, observable, and measurable learning objectives. So how can an investment realistically be determined?

Some people might suggest asking workers whether they feel they are more productive or have reduced errors in their work, and then to estimate the resulting savings. Such data is self-reported, and studies suggest that some workers tend to overestimate their learning and its impact. Using these self-reported techniques to assess the ROI of *formal* learning programs lacks credibility—and that's when learners are aware of the objectives against which they are being measured and the time frame for doing so. Such self-reported measures lack credibility even more in informal learning, when learners are not aware of their objectives or the time frame of learning.

Instead, experts suggest reporting broader data on the use of and satisfaction with informal learning, which appeals to those who feel the need to report numbers, and providing descriptive data about the impact of these efforts on individual employees. Evidence suggests that executives will find such a combination of numerical and descriptive data compelling because they are aware of the challenges in demonstrating return on this type of investment (Carliner, 2007; Marsick and Watkins, 2011; O'Driscoll, Sugrue, and Vona, 2005).

Unique Issues in Reporting the Results of Evaluation

In many ways, the considerations for reporting the results of evaluations of informal learning are the same as those for formal learning. These include

- ▶ determining how the recipients of the evaluation results intend to use them, such as validating their investments in training or determining whether to pursue a particular approach to training
- ▶ presenting the evaluation results as clearly and concisely as possible
- ▶ putting the results into the context of the audience.

In addition to these general considerations, one of the unique challenges in presenting results of evaluations of informal learning is that many people do not understand it. These people do not have a clear definition of informal learning and cannot differentiate among formal and informal learning processes.

Furthermore, stakeholders who have been trained by training and development professionals to accept evaluations following the Kirkpatrick methodology—reporting on satisfaction, learning, transfer, and impact—now have to be made to understand that the nature of informal learning does not lend itself to the same types of evaluations as formal learning.

Start the education process at the beginning of the effort to evaluate informal learning. Make stakeholders aware of the issues involved and provide a mock-up of an evaluation report that might result from the evaluation. Doing so sets stakeholder expectations early.

This also surfaces possible objections. For example, a stakeholder might comment that a proposed plan for evaluation does not report on ROI. Rather than claim this is impossible, the training and development professional might ask the stakeholder to suggest how they might track ROI. Perhaps that person will have a useful suggestion, but it is likely that he or she will be as stumped as the training and development professional. Because that stakeholder cannot devise a means of evaluating ROI, he or she can better understand the inherent difficulty in doing so.

Getting It Done

Worksheet 8–1 serves as a quick reference for you to see which evaluation methods are appropriate for the different types of evaluations you may want to conduct.

Worksheet 8–1. Matching Evaluation Needs With Methods

What you want to evaluate	Methods available to evaluate it	Which methods suit your evaluation needs and why?
Informal learning at the individual level		
Identify *what* workers learned	• Self-assessments • Process portfolios • Coaching interviews	
Identify *how* workers learned it	• Process portfolios • Coaching	
Recognize acquired competencies	• Employee education records • Skills assessments • Certifications • Badges	
Informal learning across groups of workers		
Determine the extent to which individual resources for informal learning were used	• Analytics • Compiling data from evaluations of individual learning efforts	
Assess satisfaction with individual resources	• Surveys • Focus groups	
Identify the impact of individual resources	• Rater systems • Specialized reports • Long-term studies	

How might you evaluate informal learning programs in your organization? Try the exercises in Worksheet 8–2 to find out.

Worksheet 8–2. Exercises

1. In his conversations with workers in his focus group who have fewer than 10 years' work experience, the Director of Research and Development heard several of the workers discussing mentoring. Some workers mentioned that they felt someone in the organization had meaningfully mentored them, while others felt as if no one in the organization had mentored them. The director is aware that the company has no formal mentoring program but would like for you to find out how much mentoring goes on within the organization and how workers feel about it.

   So what do you do?

   _____

   _____

   _____

   _____

   _____

   Debriefing of exercise 1: This is an example of evaluating learning at the collective level. The evaluation focuses on two issues: "How much mentoring is occurring in Research and Development?" and "What is the satisfaction with the mentoring that workers receive?"

   Two methods can provide insights into the answers. Focus groups let workers identify whether they have been mentored and how they have felt about being mentored or being overlooked in mentoring. But the data only applies to the people who participate; it does not provide insights into mentoring throughout the entire Research and Development department. An employee survey given to the group of interest—workers with 10 years or fewer of work experience—and that specifically addresses questions on mentoring—can provide numerical data on the extent of mentoring and an assessment of satisfaction with it.

   But the ideal solution might be a two-part approach. Start with a focus group to learn more about specific mentoring issues in the organization and use the insights gained there to create a survey intended for all Research and Development workers with 10 years or fewer of work experience.

2. Colleen, your colleague in the Human Resources department, has asked you to help her with a challenge. A manager and her employee disagree over the qualifications of the employee to serve as a project manager. The manager notes that the worker has not completed any formal training in project management. Although this is a preferred qualification, the responsibilities do not explicitly require it. The worker has argued that "I'm self-taught. I've read a lot about this and have practiced on my own." How can you help resolve the stalemate?

_____

_____

_____

_____

_____

Debriefing of exercise 2: This is an example of evaluating learning at the individual level. Your instinct might lead you to explore the claims of the worker that he or she has actually participated in learning. Because the worker has not yet used the skills on the job, providing a process portfolio might prove challenging. You might therefore use a coaching interview to determine how the worker studied project management and what the worker learned.

But what the worker really wants is formal recognition for the informal learning so he or she can be eligible for this new role. This chapter suggested three means of providing recognition. The first would involve adding the informal learning to the employee education record. But because the worker claims to have studied on his or her own, any data entered into the system could not be verified. A skills assessment, specifically focused on management skills, would provide more specific feedback. But in the end, it's just self-reported data with no evidence to support the claim. That leaves certification, which involves demonstrating competence to a third party. By choosing certification, the argument changes from "the worker feels qualified, the manager feels otherwise" to "in the eyes of an independent third party, the qualifications of this worker are. . . ."

References & Resources

■ ■

Introduction

Ackerman, D. (1993). Slices of Life. *Discover* 14(11): 102–104.

Bornstein, D. (2010). The Plan to Make Homelessness History. *New York Times* online, December 20, 2010. Viewed at http://opinionator.blogs.nytimes.com/2010/12/20/a-plan-to-make-homelessness-history/. Visited December 27, 2010.

Carliner, S. (1998). How Designers Make Decisions: A Descriptive Model of Instructional Design for Informal Learning in Museums. *Performance Improvement Quarterly* 11(2): 72–92.

Csikzentmihalyi, M., and K. Hermanson. (1995). Intrinsic Motivation in Museums: What Makes Visitors Want to Learn? *Museum News* 74(3): 35–37, 59–62.

Tracey, R. (2010). *My Award-Winning IQ.* E-Learning Provocateur blog. June 11, 2010. Viewed at http://ryan2point0.wordpress.com/2010/06/10/my-award-winning-iq/. Visited January 7, 2011.

Chapter 1

Aguinis, H., and K. Kraiger. (2009). Benefits of Training and Development for Individuals and Teams, Organizations, and Society. *Annual Review of Psychology* 60: 451–474.

Bloom, J., and E.A. Powell. (1984). *Museums for a New Century: A Report of the Commission on Museums for a New Century.* Washington, DC: American Association of Museums.

Bloom, M. (2009). Learning and Development: The Skills-Training Disconnect. *Inside Edge.* Viewed at http://www.conferenceboard.ca/insideedge/2009/august-2009/aug17-vp-corner.aspx. Visited January 23, 2012.

Broad, M.L., and J.W. Newstrom. (2001). *Transfer of Training: Action-Packed Strategies to Ensure High Payoff From Training Investments.* New York: Perseus Books.

Burk, L.A., and H.M. Hutchins. (2007). Training Transfer: An Integrative Literature Review. *Human Resource Development Review* 6(3): 263–296.

Cappelli, P. (2008). *Talent on Demand: Managing Talent in an Age of Uncertainty.* Cambridge, MA: Harvard Business Press.

Carliner, S. (1995). *Every Object Tells a Story: A Grounded Model of Design for Object-Based Learning in Museums.* Unpublished doctoral dissertation. Atlanta: Georgia State University.

Carliner, S. (2000). *Eight Things That Training and Performance Improvement Professionals Must Know About Knowledge Management.* Published online. Minneapolis, MN: VNU Business Media.

Carliner, S., and I. Bakir. (2010). Trends in Spending on Training: An Analysis of the 1982 Through 2008 Training Annual Industry Survey Reports. *Performance Improvement Quarterly* 23(3): 77–105.

Carter, S.D. (2005). The Growth of Supply and Demand of Occupational-Based Training and Certification in the United States, 1990–2003. *Human Resource Development Quarterly* 16(1): 33–54.

Colley, H., P. Hodkinson, and J. Malcolm. (2003). Understanding Informality and Formality in Learning. *Adult Learning* 15(3): 7–9.

Cross, J. (2007). *Informal Learning: Rediscovering the Natural Pathways That Inspire Innovation and Performance.* San Francisco: Pfeiffer.

Driscoll, M., and S. Carliner. (2005). *Advanced Web-Based Training: Adapting Real World Strategies in Your Online Learning.* San Francisco: Pfeiffer.

"Edutainment." (2010). Wikipedia. Viewed at http://en.wikipedia.org/wiki/Edutainment. Visited January 3, 2011.

Gery, G. (1991). *Electronic Performance Support Systems.* Tolland, MA: Gery Performance Press, Inc.

Gibbons, M. (2002). *The Self-Directed Learning Handbook.* San Francisco: Jossey-Bass.

Gibbons, M. (2008). "What Is Self-Directed Learning?" Viewed at www.selfdirectedlearning.com. Visited December 11, 2010.

Gilbert, T. (1978). *Human Competence: Engineering Worthy Performance.* New York: McGraw-Hill.

Hager, P. (2004). Lifelong Learning in the Workplace? Challenges and Issues. *Journal of Workplace Learning* 16(1–2): 22–32.

Jacobs, R.L., and Y. Park. (2009). A Proposed Conceptual Framework of Workplace Learning: Implications for Theory Development and Research in Human Resource Development. *Human Resource Development Review* 8(2): 133–150.

Lalonde, D. (2010). "Sondage AQIII 2010: La formation continue negligee." Direction Informatique. Viewed at http://www.linkedin.com/news?viewArticle=&articleID=22 3052599&gid=3254662&type=member&item=32053081&articleURL=http://www. directioninformatique.com/DI/client/fr/DirectionInformatique/Nouvelles.asp%3Fid %3D59624%26cid%3D79&urlhash=DQ62. Visited November 26, 2010.

Livingstone, D. (2010). *The Relationship Between Workers' Practical Knowledge and Their Job Requirements: Findings of the 1998, 2004 and 2010 National Surveys of Work and Lifelong Learning*. 2010 Canadian Society for Training and Development Conference. Toronto, ON, November 17, 2010.

Marsick, V.J. (2009). Toward a Unifying Framework to Support Informal Learning Theory, Research and Practice. *Journal of Workplace Learning* 21(4): 265–275.

Merriam, S.B. (ed.). (2001). *The New Update on Adult Learning Theory*. San Francisco: Jossey-Bass.

Ogata, H., and Y. Yanno. (2004). "Context-Aware Support for Computer-Supported Ubiquitous Learning." Viewed at http://www-yano.is.tokushima-u.ac.jp/ogata/clue/ WMTE-03-1-50.pdf. Visited January 10, 2010.

Oregon Sea Grant. (2004). "Developing the Art and Science of Free-Choice Learning." Viewed at http://seagrant.oregonstate.edu/makingadifference/stories/Free_ ChoiceSoA.pdf. Visited January 3, 2011.

Schulz, M., and C.S. Rosznagel. (2010). Informal Workplace Learning: An Exploration of Age Differences in Learning Competence. *Learning and Instruction* 20(5): 383–399.

Selwyn, N. (2010). *The Educational Significance of Social Media*. Toronto, ON: Association for the Advancement of Computers in Education.

Werquin, P. (2007). Moving Mountains: Will Qualifications Systems Promote Lifelong Learning? *European Journal of Education* 42(4): 459–484.

Wihak, C., G. Hall, J. Bratton, L. Warkentin, L. Wihak, and S. MacPherson. (2008). *Work-Related Informal Learning: Research and Practice in the Canadian Context*. Unpublished report. Ottawa, ON: Work and Learning Knowledge Centre of the Canadian Centre for Learning.

Chapter 2

Aral, S. (2010). *Content Is King: Combining Network and Text Analysis.* Presented at the 2010 meeting of the Academy of Management, Montreal, QC, August 9, 2010.

Bennett, S., K. Maton, and L. Kervin. (2008). The "Digital Natives" Debate: A Critical Review of the Evidence. *British Journal of Educational Technology* 39(5): 775–786.

Broad, M.L., and J.W. Newstrom. (2001). *Transfer of Training: Action-Packed Strategies to Ensure High Payoff From Training Investments.* New York: Perseus Books.

Burke, L.A., and H.M. Hutchins. (2007). Training Transfer: An Integrative Literature Review. *Human Resource Development Review* 6(3): 263–296.

Carliner, S., and C. Bernard. (2011a). *An Integrative Review of Literature on the Perceptions of HRD.* Proceedings of the 2011 Academy of Human Resource Development Research Conference in the Americas. St. Paul, MN: Academy of Human Resource Development.

Carliner, S., and C. Bernard. (2011b). *A Qualitative Study of the Perceptions of Workplace Learning Professionals.* 2011 Joint Canadian Society for the Study of Adult Education and the Adult Education Research Conferences, Toronto, ON, June 9, 2011.

Carliner, S., R. Legassie, S. Belding, H. MacDonald, O. Ribeiro, L. Johnston, J. MacDonald, and H. Hein. (2009). How Research Moves Into Practice: A Preliminary Study of What Training Professionals Read, Hear, and Perceive. *Canadian Journal of Learning and Technology* 35(1). Viewed at http://www.cjlt.ca/index.php/cjlt/article/view/510/240. Visited December 26, 2009.

Clark, R. (2010). Closing Keynote. 2010 Association for Educational Communications and Technology International Convention, Anaheim, CA, October 29, 2010.

Cross, J. (2007). *Informal Learning: Rediscovering the Natural Pathways That Inspire Innovation and Performance.* San Francisco: Pfeiffer.

Dale, M., and J. Bell. (1999). *Informal Learning in the Workplace.* Research Brief No. 134. UK Department for Education and Employment.

Dick, W., L. Carey, and J. Carey. (2008). *The Systematic Design of Instruction,* 7th edition. Burlington, MA: Addison-Wesley.

Downing, J. (2006). Using Customer Contact Center Technicians to Measure the Effectiveness of Online Help Systems. *Technical Communication* 54(2): 201–209.

Edvisson, L., and M.S. Malone. (1997). *Intellectual Capital: Realizing Your Company's True Value by Finding Its Hidden Brainpower.* New York: HarperCollins.

Ellinger, A.D. (2005). Contextual Factors Influencing Informal Learning in a Workplace Setting: The Case of "Reinventing Itself Company." *Human Resource Development Quarterly* 16(3): 389–415.

Falk, J.H., and L. Dierking. (2000). *Learning From Museums: Visitor Experiences and the Making of Meaning*. Walnut Creek, CA: AltaMira Press.

Kay, R. (2007). A Formative Analysis of Resources Used to Learn Software. *Canadian Journal of Learning and Technology* 33(1). Viewed at http://www.cjlt.ca/index.php/cjlt/article/view/20/18. Visited March 19, 2011.

Knowles, M., R.A. Swanson, and E.F. Holton. (2011). *The Adult Learner*, 7th ed. Burlington, MA: Butterworth-Heinemann.

Kristof, N.D. (2009). Learning How to Think. *New York Times*. Viewed at http://www.nytimes.com/2009/03/26/opinion/26Kristof.html?ref=opinion. Visited March 26, 2009.

Laiken, M., K. Edge, S. Friedman, and K. West. (2008). *Formalizing the Informal: From Informal to Organizational Learning in the Post-Industrial Workplace*. New York: Springer.

Lim, D.H., and M.L. Morris. (2006). Influence of Trainee Characteristics, Instructional Satisfaction, and Organizational Climate on Perceived Learning and Training Transfer. *Human Resource Development Quarterly* 17(1): 85–115.

Mager, R. (1997). *Preparing Instructional Objectives*. Atlanta, GA: Center for Effective Performance.

Marsick, V.J. (2009). Toward a Unifying Framework to Support Informal Learning Theory, Research and Practice. *Journal of Workplace Learning* 21(4): 265–275.

Marsick, V.J., and K. Watkins. (1990). *Informal and Incidental Learning in the Workplace*. London, UK: Routledge.

Marsick, V.J., and K.E. Watkins. (2001). Chapter 3: Informal and Incidential Learning. In *The New Update on Adult Learning Theory*, ed. S.B. Merriam. San Francisco: Jossey-Bass.

Marsick, V.J., and K. Watkins. (2011). *Pursuing Research in Organizations That Is Useful to Practice*. Academy of Human Resource Development Research Conference in the Americas, Schaumberg, IL.

Merriam, S.B. (2001). Editor's notes. In *The New Update on Adult Learning Theory*, ed. S.B. Merriam. San Francisco: Jossey-Bass.

Millar, R.P. (2008). *Informal Learning in the Workplace*. Third Annual Symposium of the Work and Learning Knowledge Centre. Canadian Council on Learning, Ottawa, ON.

Skule, S. (2004). Learning Conditions at Work: A Framework to Understand and Assess Informal Learning in the Workplace. *International Journal of Training and Development* 8(1): 8–20.

Wedman, J., and M. Tessmer. (1993). Instructional Designer's Decisions and Priorities: A Survey of Design Practice. *Performance Improvement Quarterly* 6(2): 43–57.

Westbrook, T.S., and J.R. Veale. (2001). Work-Related Learning as a Core Value: An Iowa Perspective. *Human Resource Development Quarterly* 12(3): 301–317.

Zemke, R., and C. Lee. (1987). How Long Does It Take? *TRAINING* 24(6): 75–80.

Chapter 3

Brooks, D. (2011). The Modesty Manifest. *New York Times*, March 10, 2011. Viewed at http://www.nytimes.com/2011/03/11/opinion/11brooks.html?_r=1&src=me&ref=homepage. Visited March 11, 2011.

Cseh, M., K.E. Watkins, and V.J. Marsick. (1999). Re-Conceptualizing Marsick and Watkins' Model of Informal and Incidental Learning in the Workplace. In *Proceedings, Academy of Human Resource Development Conference*, vol. 1, ed. K.P. Kuchinke. Baton Rouge, LA: Academy of Human Resource Development.

Eraut, M. (2000). Non-Formal Learning and Tacit Knowledge in Professional Work. *British Journal of Educational Psychology* 70(1): 113–136.

Livingstone, D. (2010). *The Relationship Between Workers' Practical Knowledge and Their Job Requirements: Findings of the 1998, 2004, and 2010 National Surveys of Work and Lifelong Learning*. Presented at the Canadian Society for Training and Development Annual Conference and Trade Show, Toronto, ON, November 17, 2010.

Chapter 4

ASTD. (2010). The ASTD WLP Competency Model. Viewed at http://www.astd.org/content/research/competency/AreasofExpertise.htm. Visited November 5, 2011.

Bloom, M., D. Watt, D. Hughes, D. Munro, J. Stuckey, Z. Sleiman, and C. Charman. (2011). *Knowledge Gathering Project: Work-Related Learning in SMEs: Effective Programs*. Presentation to the Centre for Workplace Skills, Ottawa, ON, May 12, 2011.

Carliner, S. (2000). Physical, Cognitive, and Affective: A Three-Part Framework for Information Design. *Technical Communication* 47(4): 561–576.

Carliner, S., A. Qayyum, J.C. Sanchez-Lozano, and S. Macmillan. (2007). *The Value of Training: What Training Managers Track, What Training Managers Report*. Academy of Human Resource Development International Research Conference, Indianapolis, IN, March 3, 2007.

Downing, J. (2006). Using Customer Contact Center Technicians to Measure the Effectiveness of Online Help Systems. *Technical Communication* 54(2): 201–209.

Eraut, M. (2000). Non-Formal Learning and Tacit Knowledge in Professional Work. *British Journal of Educational Psychology* 70(1): 113–136.

Kolb, D. (1984). *Experiential Learning*. Englewood Cliffs, NJ: Prentice Hall.

Leigh, D., and R. Watkins. (2005). E-Learner Success: Validating a Self-Assessment of Learner Readiness for Online Training. In *Proceedings of the 2005 ASTD Research-to-Practice Conference-Within-a-Conference*, ed. S. Carliner and B. Sugrue. Alexandria, VA: ASTD Press.

Marsick, V.J., and K. Watkins. (1990). *Informal and Incidental Learning in the Workplace*. London, UK: Routledge.

Marsick, V.J., and K. Watkins. (2011). *Pursuing Research in Organizations That Is Useful to Practice*. Academy of Human Resource Development Research Conference in the Americas, Schaumberg, IL, February 24, 2011.

M.E.M. C.C.A.S.T.D. (2010). Chicagoland Chapter (CC) ASTD webinar with Bob Mosher. Informal Learning: Are We Missing a HUGE Opportunity? Viewed at http://vimeo.com/14435510. Visited June 2, 2011.

O'Driscoll, T., B. Sugrue, and M.K. Vona. (2005). The C-Level and the Value of Learning. *Training + Development* 59(10): 70–78.

Sitzmann, T., B.S. Bell, K. Kraiger, and A.M. Kanar. (2009). A Multilevel Analysis of the Effect of Prompting Self-Regulation in Technology-Delivered Instruction. *Personnel Psychology* 62(4): 697–734.

Sitzmann, T., K. Ely, B.S. Bell, and K. Bauer. (2008). *A Multilevel Analysis of the Effects of Technical Interruptions on Learning and Attrition From Web-Based Instruction* (CAHRS Working Paper No. 08-11). Ithaca, NY: Cornell University, School of Industrial and Labor Relations, Center for Advanced Human Resource Studies. http://digitalcommons.ilr.cornell.edu/cahrswp/490.

Sitzmann, T., K. Ely, K.G. Brown, and K. Bauer. (2008). Self-Assessment of Knowledge: A Cognitive Learning or Affective Measure? *Academy of Management Learning and Education* 9(2): 169–191.

Chapter 5

Driscoll, M., and S. Carliner. (2005). *Advanced Web-Based Training: Adapting Real World Strategies in Your Online Learning*. San Francisco: Pfeiffer.

Klingensmith, K. (2009). *PLN: Your Personal Learning Network Made Easy*. Once a Teacher blog. Viewed at http://onceateacher.wordpress.com/2009/05/05/pln-your-personal-learning-network-made-easy/. Published May 5, 2009. Visited April 15, 2011.

Laiken, M., K. Edge, S. Friedman, and K. West. (in press). Formalizing the Informal: From Informal to Organizational Learning in the Post-industrial Workplace. In *Making Sense of Lived Experience in Turbulent Times: Informal Learning*, ed. K. Church, E. Shragge, and N. Bascia. New York: Springer.

Poell, R., G.E. Chivers, F.J. Van Der Krogt, and D.A. Wildemeersc. (2000). Learning-Network Theory: Organizing the Dynamic Relationships Between Learning and Work. *Management Learning* 31(1): 25–49.

Sproull, L., and S. Kiesler. (1991). *Connections: New Ways of Working in the Networked Organization*. Cambridge, MA: MIT Press.

U.S. Office of Personnel Management. (2008). Best Practices: Mentoring. U.S. Office of Personnel Management. Viewed at http://www.opm.gov/hrd/lead/BestPractices-Mentoring.pdf. Visited May 4, 2011.

Chapter 6

Bennett, S., K. Maton, and L. Kervin. (2008). The "Digital Natives" Debate: A Critical Review of the Evidence. *British Journal of Educational Technology* 39(5): 775–786.

Chapman, B. (2010). *How Long Does It Take to Create Learning?* Chapman Alliance. Viewed at http://www.chapmanalliance.com/howlong/. Visited January 9, 2012.

Downing, J. (2006). Using Customer Contact Center Technicians to Measure the Effectiveness of Online Help Systems. *Technical Communication* 54(2): 201–209.

Gery, G. (1991). *Electronic Performance Support Systems*. Tolland, MA: Gery Performance Press.

Jacobson, D. (n.d.). Making the Most of Developmental Assignments: Q&A With Author Cynthia McCauley. GovernmentLeaders.org. Viewed at http://govleaders.org/development.htm. Visited May 9, 2011.

Leland, J. (2008). Simulating Age 85, With Lessons on Offering Care. *New York Times*, August 3, 2008. Viewed at http://www.nytimes.com/2008/08/03/us/03aging.html?em=&pagewanted=all. Visited August 4, 2008.

Lemelson-MIT Program. (n.d.). *Arthur Fry & Spencer Silver*. Inventor of the Week Archive. Viewed at http://web.mit.edu/invent/iow/frysilver.html. Visited May 19, 2011.

McCauley, C. (1958). *Developmental Assignments: Creating Learning Experiences Without Changing Jobs*. Greensboro, NC: Center for Creative Leadership.

Service Canada. (n.d.). Video Centre: Training and Development Service Canada website. Viewed at http://www.servicecanada.gc.ca/eng/video/td.shtml. Visited May 9, 2011.

Storify. (2010). Storify Overview. YouTube. Viewed at http://www.youtube.com/watch?v=CV0AlJNBONs&feature=player_embedded#at=48. Visited May 9, 2011.

Sullenberger, C.B., and J. Zaslow. (2010). *Highest Duty: My Search for What Really Matters*. New York: Harper.

Swanson, R.A., and J.A. Zuber. (1996). A Case Study of a Failed Organization Development Intervention Rooted in the Employee Survey Process. *Performance Improvement Quarterly* 9(2): 42–56.

Vosecky, T., M. Siegel, and C. Wallace. (2008). Making and Acting: Ethnographic Development of a Case Study Approach. *Technical Communication* 55(4): 405–424.

Wikipedia. (2011). Post-it Note. Viewed at http://en.wikipedia.org/wiki/Post-it. Visited May 19, 2011.

Yip, A. (2005). *CSI Hong Kong: Anatomy of an E-Learning Program*. ASTD International Conference and Exposition, Orlando, FL, June 5, 2005.

Chapter 7

Carliner, S. (2005). E-Portfolios: The Tool That Can Increase Your Marketability and Refine Your Skill Development Efforts. *T&D* May: 71–74.

Downes, S. (2006). *PLE diagram*. Half an Hour blog. Viewed at http://halfanhour. blogspot.com/2006/10/ple-diagram.html. Visited September 23, 2011.

Freeman, W. (2010). Canadian Society for the Study of Discourse and Writing Conference, Montreal, QC, May 31, 2010.

The Horizon Report. (2007). *Collaboration Between the New Media Consortium and the Educause Learning Initiative*. Viewed at http://www.nmc.org/pdf/2007_Horizon_ Report.pdf. Visited January 25, 2007.

Rossett, A., and J. Marshall. (2010). What's Old Is New Again. *T+D* January. Viewed at http://www.astd.org/TD/Archives/2010/Jan/Free/1001_eLearning_Whats_Old.htm. Visited September 23, 2011.

Shank, P. (2008). Chapter 8: Web 2.0 and Beyond: The Changing Needs of Learners, New Tools, and Ways to Learn. In *The E-Learning Handbook: Past Promises, Present Challenges*, ed. S. Carliner and P. Shank. San Francisco: Pfeiffer.

Chapter 8

Arthur, W., W. Bennet, P.S. Edens, and S.T. Bell. (2003). Effectiveness of Training in Organizations: A Meta-Analysis of Design and Evaluation Features. *Journal of Applied Psychology* 88(2): 234–245.

Brown, K.G. (2005). Examining the Structure and Nomological Network of Trainee Reactions: A Closer Look at "Smile Sheets." *Journal of Applied Psychology*, 90: 991–1001.

Carliner, S. (2005). E-Portfolios: A Different Type of E-Learning Tool. *Training & Development* 59(5): 71–74.

Carliner, S. (2007). *The Value of Training: What Training Managers Track, What Training Managers Report*. Proceedings of the 2007 Academy of Human Resource Development Conference.

Kirkpatrick, D.L. (1994). *Evaluating Training Programs: The Four Levels*. San Francisco: Berrett-Koehler.

Marsick, V.J., and K. Watkins. (2011). *Pursuing Research in Organizations That Is Useful to Practice*. Academy of Human Resource Development Research Conference in the Americas, Schaumberg, IL, February 24, 2011.

O'Driscoll, T., B. Sugrue, and M.K. Vona. (2005). The C-Level and the Value of Learning. *Training + Development* 59(10): 70–78.

Teja, F. (2011). Thinking Out of the Box: How the University of British Columbia School of Nursing Created a Practice e-Portfolio. *Learning Solutions Magazine*, February 23, 2011. Viewed at http://www.learningsolutionsmag.com/articles/421/ thinking-out-of-the-box-how-the-university-of-british-columbia-school-of-nursing-created-a-practice-e-portfolio. Visited February 28, 2011.

Tharenou, P., A.M. Saks, and C. Moore. (2007). A Review and Critique of Research on Training and Organizational-Level Outcomes. *Human Resource Management Review* 17(3): 251–273.

Trademarks Used

Android is a trademark of Google, Inc.

Connect is a trademark of Adobe Corporation.

Flash and Dreamweaver are registered trademarks of Adobe Corporation.

Galaxy is a trademark of Samsung Corporation.

iPad is a registered trademark of Apple Corporation.

LinkedIn is a registered trademark of LinkedIn Corporation.

WebEx is a registered trademark of Cisco Corporation.

Wikipedia is a registered trademark of WikiCommons.

Wordpress is a registered trademark of the Wordpress Foundation.

YouTube is a registered trademark of Google Corporation.

About the Author

Saul Carliner is Director of the Education Doctoral Program and an associate professor at Concordia University in Montreal. His research and teaching focus on the design of emerging forms of online learning and communication for the workplace, and management issues that arise when producing these materials. Also an industry consultant, he has provided strategic planning and evaluation services for organizations in Africa, Asia, Australia, North America, and Europe, including Alltel Wireless, AT&T, Equitas, IBM, Microsoft, ST Microelectronics Turkish Management Centre, Wachovia, and several US and Canadian government agencies. Among 150 articles and 7 other books are the best-selling Training Design Basics (ASTD Press) and Designing e-Learning, and award-winning e-Learning Handbook (with Patti Shank, Pfeiffer). A Certified Training and Development Professional, he is a member of the board of the Canadian Society for Training and Development, a past Research Fellow of ASTD, and a Fellow and past international president of the Society for Technical Communication. He holds degrees from Carnegie Mellon University, University of Minnesota, and Georgia State University.

Index

In this index, *f* represents a figure; *t* represents a table

A

accountability, 174–175
    See also return-on-investment (ROI)
adult learning, 7*f*, 14, 26
advertising, 131
affective objectives, 22
agile development, 23–24
Amazon.com, 193
analytics, 178*t*, 186–188
apprenticeships, 7*f*, 105
Aral, Sinan, 30
articles, academic/professional, 24
assessment. *See* evaluation
ASTD Competency Model, 62–63*f*
audio recordings, 157*t*
audiovisual equipment, 155*t*

B

badges, learning, 178*t*, 185, 196
behaviorism, 32, 93, 112
Bell, John, 20, 23, 27

Bernard, Colleen, 22
blogs, 9, 30, 107, 142, 162*t*, 165
    microblogs, 9, 163*t*
book groups, 108
brainstorming, 82, 85–86

C

career assessment, 50
career development plan, 73
career goals, choosing, 49–51
case studies, 24, 132–133*f*
certifications, 11, 73, 178*t*, 185, 188
Certified Professional in Learning and
        Performance (CPLP), 62, 73
chat, electronic, 160*t*
Clark, Richard, 28
classic media, 157*t*–158*t*
Client Logic, 139
cloud computing, 68
coaching
    coach role, 61
    competency, 62–63
    developmental assignments, 121